THE AGE OF UNREASON

Charles Handy is an independent writer, teacher and broadcaster, known to many for his 'Thoughts for Today' on the BBC's *Today* programme. He has been in his time, an oil executive, an economist, a professor at the London Business School, the Warden of St George's House at Windsor Castle and the chairman of the Royal Society for the Encouragement of Arts, Manufacture and Commerce. He was named Business Columnist of the Year in 1994.

Charles Handy was born in Kildare in Ireland, the son of an Archdeacon, and educated in Ireland, England (Oxford University) and the USA (Massachusetts Institute of Technology).

His other books published by Arrow include *The Elephant and the Flea*, *The Hungry Spirit*, *The Empty Raincoat*, *Waiting for the Mountain to Move*, *Beyond Certainty*, *Gods of Management* and *Understanding Organizations*.

He and his wife Elizabeth, a portrait photographer, live in London, Norfolk and Tuscany.

By the same author

The Elephant and the Flea
The Empty Raincoat
The Hungry Spirit
Gods of Management
Waiting for the Mountain to Move
Understand Organizations
Understanding Schools as Organizations
Understanding Voluntary Organizations
Inside Organizations
Beyond Certainty: the Changing Worlds of Organizations

THE AGE OF
UNREASON

CHARLES HANDY

ARROW

Published by Arrow in 2002

9 10 8

Copyright © 1989, 1991 by Charles Handy

Charles Handy has asserted his right under the Copyright, Designs
and Patents Act, 1988 to be identified as the author of this work

First published by Random House Business Books in 1989

Arrow
The Random House Group Limited
20 Vauxhall Bridge Road, London SW1V 2SA

Random House Australia (Pty) Limited
20 Alfred Street, Milsons Point, Sydney,
New South Wales 2061, Australia

Random House New Zealand Limited
18 Poland Road, Glenfield,
Auckland 10, New Zealand

Random House (Pty) Limited
Endulini, 5a Jubilee Road, Parktown 2193, South Africa

The Random House Group Limited Reg. No. 954009

www.randomhouse.co.uk

A CIP catalogue record for this book
is available from the British Library

Papers used by Random House are natural, recyclable
products made from wood grown in sustainable forests.
The manufacturing processes conform to the
environmental regulations of the country of origin.

ISBN 0 0995 4831 3

Printed and bound in Denmark by
Nørhaven Paperback A/S, Viborg

Contents

Contents

Acknowledgements

The future is not inevitable. We can influence it, if we know what we want it to be. That conviction is the reason for this book. We can and should be in charge of our own destinies in a time of change.

The book, in part, builds on my previous writings: on organizations, on the future of work, on schools and voluntary organizations, on middle-age and on religion. They all, I now realize, hang together as different parts and parcels of life. To separate them out was to collude with the besetting sin of modern life, reductionism, reducing things to their component parts and thereby too often, missing the meaning and message of the wood in a minute examination of its trees.

The book is addressed primarily to those who work in and who manage organizations or some part of them, because it is their hands that rest on the levers of change, although they may not always realize it. The changes which we are already seeing in our lives, and which we will see more of, have their origins in the changes in our workplaces. Work has always been the major influence on the way we live. It still is, but often in unexpected ways.

The ideas in the book come from many sources, only some of which I have been able to acknowledge specifically in the text. The managers, and others whom I meet in seminars, courses and conferences around the world have contributed many of them, and a group of young executives drawn together by Hay Management Consultants in 1988 to look at the world ahead of them was particularly stimulating. Peter Drucker's thoughts on the *Age of Disconti-*

nuity and Tom Peters' on *A World Turned Upside-Down* anticipated two of the major themes of the book. They were talking about organizations. I think it goes much farther than that.

Without the encouragement, and the deadlines, of my publishers, Gail Rebuck and Lucy Shankleman, this book would not have happened. I am very grateful to them for their perceptive comments and their belief in the book. Elizabeth, my wife and partner, has lived with every line of this book, on the page and in our life together. I applaud the generosity with which she has tolerated this writing through living and all the help she has given me. Writing the book was my way of beginning to take charge of my destiny: I hope that reading it will help others to do the same.

Charles Handy,
Diss, Norfolk,
England.

Preface to the second edition

I was in Dresden not so long ago, in what we must now call *Eastern* Germany. Herr Motte is the man responsible for returning to private ownership the 700 or so business corporations that were, until 1991, owned and controlled by the state in that area. He had a staff of 32 and needed to sell one or two corporations *every* day to meet his target, with many of them literally unsaleable. It is a formidable task and I asked him where he looked for guidance. 'In reshaping the business sector of Eastern Germany,' he said 'there are no models. We have to re-shape the future.'

When this book was first published that wall which divided East from West was a permanent obstacle to peace. Within six months it was gone; a dramatic example of the discontinuous change which was the excuse for the book. Herr Motte's answer to me was also the perfect summary of how we must respond, not by looking to the past but by creating something new, different and hopefully better, by being 'unreasonable' in the sense in which George Bernard Shaw meant the word, by thinking unconventionally, even upside-down.

The book is about work and about individual lives, not about politics and wars and countries, but the messages are the same and the changes just as dramatic. As this edition goes to press there are fears of widespread recession. Part of that recession will be because our organizations have become too expensive, too complicated and cumbersome. Like the centrally planned economies of the old communist world these centrally planned organizations are also discovering, rather late in the day, that the old ways which worked quite well in the past are no longer cost-effective. They will have to re-shape their futures and re-think the way they get work done if they are going to survive in an age when technology makes almost anything possible.

The answers will affect us all. All over America, on a recent trip, I saw splendid new office towers in the downtown city areas. No lights shone there, however, because no-one was in them. Recession? Or a big re-think about the need for expensive offices in the new organizations? We shall have to wait and see.

I have not changed my views since the first edition came out, about the way the world of work is heading and the ways we need to respond, although I have updated some of the numbers and the examples. Nor do many people seem to disagree, in broad principle, with these views although they may argue about the detail and the timing. For most, however, it is a depressing prospect, one of a tide of history going out carrying with it a lot of dead fish, driftwood and garbage. For me, it is a tide coming in, full of opportunities for new launches and some re-floatings. Incoming tides can also, of course, swamp the unsuspecting and the unready and I still worry about the hordes I see pouring off the commuter trains every morning who seem to think, or hope, that they live by a tideless and unchanging sea.

They don't. Nor do these tides keep to neat tables. They come in surges. It is truly an age of uncertainty and of unreason. Like it or not we shall have to live in it, and most of us, for much of our now longer lives, will live in it outside those comfortable prisons which we called organizations and which provided the structure for our days and years.

That new freedom is the most significant bit of discontinuous change for most of us. But as the new democracies of Eastern Europe are finding, freedom can be very uncomfortable. I believe that there is no choice. The old ways of work are gone; we have to re-shape our futures. A lot hinges on those who will lead and design the new organizations. They, not our politicians, are the makers of our destinies and it is to them that this book is mainly directed in the hope that they may have the vision and the courage to be sensibly unreasonable.

Charles Handy,
Hiss, Norfolk,
England,
1991.

Part One: Changing

1 The Argument

The scene was the General Synod of the Church of England in the 1980s. The topic being debated was the controversial proposition that women be admitted to the priesthood. A speaker from the floor of the Chamber spoke with passion, 'In this matter,' he cried, 'as in so much else in our great country, why cannot the status quo be the way forward?'

It was the heartfelt plea not only of the traditionalists in that Church but of those in power, anywhere, throughout the ages. If change there has to be let it be more of the same, continuous change. That way, the cynic might observe, nothing changes very much.

Continuous change is comfortable change. The past is then the guide to the future. An American friend, visiting Britain and Europe for the first time wondered, 'Why is it that over here whenever I ask the reason for anything, any institution or ceremony or set of rules, they always give me an historical answer – because ..., whereas in my country we always want a functional answer – in order to ...' Europeans, I suggested, look backwards to the best of their history and change as little as they can; Americans look forward and want to change as much as they may.

Circumstances do, however, combine occasionally to discomfort the advocates of the status quo. Wars, of course, are the great discomforters, but so is technology, when it takes one of its leaps forward as it did in the Industrial Revolution, so is demography, when it throws up baby booms or busts, so is a changing set of values, like that which occurred during the student unrest of 1968, and so are economics.

Circumstances are now once again, I believe, combining in curious ways. Change is not what it used to be. The status quo will no longer be the best way forward. That way will be less comfortable and less easy but, no doubt, more interesting – a word we often use to signal an uncertain mix of danger and opportunity. If we wish to enjoy more of the opportunity and less of the risk we need to understand the changes better. Those who know why changes come waste less effort in protecting themselves or in fighting the inevitable. Those who realize where changes are heading are better able to use those changes to their own advantage. The society which welcomes change can use that change instead of just reacting to it.

George Bernard Shaw once observed that all progress depends on the unreasonable man. His argument was that the reasonable man adapts himself to the world while the unreasonable persists in trying to adapt the world to himself, therefore for any change of consequence we must look to the unreasonable man, or, I must add, to the unreasonable woman.

In that sense we are entering an Age of Unreason, when the future, in so many areas, is there to be shaped, by us and for us; a time when the only prediction that will hold true is that no predictions will hold true; a time, therefore, for bold imaginings in private life as well as public, for thinking the unlikely and doing the unreasonable.

That, then, is the purpose of this book – to understand better the changes which are already about us in order that we may, as individuals and as a society, suffer less and profit more. Change, after all, is only another word for growth, another synonym for learning. We can all do it, and enjoy it, if we want to.

The story or argument of this book rests on three assumptions:

— that the changes are different this time: they are discontinuous and not part of a pattern; that such discontinuity happens from time to time in history, although it is confusing and disturbing, particularly to those in power;

— that it is the little changes which can in fact make the biggest differences to our lives, even if these go unnoticed at the time, and that it is the changes in the way our *work* is organized which will make the biggest differences to the way we all will *live*.

— that discontinuous change requires discontinuous upside-down thinking to deal with it, even if both thinkers and thoughts appear absurd at first sight.

Change Is Not What It Used To Be

Thirty years ago I started work in a world-famous multinational company. By way of encouragement they produced an outline of my future career – 'This will be your life,' they said, 'with titles of likely jobs.' The line ended, I remember, with myself as chief executive of a particular company in a particular far-off country. I was, at the time, suitably flattered. I left them long before I reached the heights they planned for me, but already I knew that not only did the job they had picked out no longer exist, neither did the company I would have directed nor even the country in which I was to have operated.

Thirty years ago I thought that life would be one long continuous line, sloping upwards with luck. Today I know better. Thirty years ago that company saw the future as largely predictable, to be planned for and managed. Today they are less certain. Thirty years ago most people thought that change would mean more of the same, only better. That was incremental change and to be welcomed. Today we know that in many areas of life we cannot guarantee more of the same, be it work or money, peace or freedom, health or happiness, and cannot even predict with confidence what will be happening in our own lives. Change is now more chancy, but also more exciting if we want to see it that way.

Change has, of course, always been what we choose to make it, good or bad, trivial or crucial. Take, for instance, the one word 'change' and consider how we use it. Can any other word be asked to do so many things?

'Change is part of life' (a noun universal)
'There is a change in the arrangements' (a noun particular)
'Please count your change' (a noun metaphorical)
'Please change this wheel' (a verb transitive)
'I will not change' (a verb intransitive)
'Where do I change trains?' (a verb metaphorical)
'She is a clever change agent' (an adjective)

Where the same word is used to describe the trivial (a change of clothes) and the profound ('a change of life'), how can we easily distinguish whether it is heralding something important or not? When the same word can mean 'progress' and 'inconsistency', how should we know which is which? We might well ask whether the English language was devised to confuse the foreigner, or ourselves?

More of the same only better, and, if possible, for more people. It was a comfortable view of change, one which, in the growth-heady days of the sixties and seventies allowed so many to marry idealism to their personal prosperity. It allowed the big to grow bigger, the powerful to look forward to more power, and even the dispossessed to hope for some share of the action one day. It was a view of change which upset no one. The only trouble was that it did not work, it never has worked anywhere for very long, and even those societies in which it has seemed to be working, Japan, Germany and, perhaps, the USA are about to see that it does not work for ever. In each of those societies it is now increasingly relevant to ask 'what is the next trick?' because the current one shows every sign of ending.

It is not just because the pace of change has speeded up, which it has done, of course. We must all, sometime, have seen one of those graphs comparing, say, the speed of travel in 500 BC and every 100 years thereafter, with the line suddenly zooming upwards ever steeper in the last inch or two of the chart as we approached modern times, when horses are superceded by cars, then by planes and then by rockets. Faster change on its own sits quite comfortably with the 'more only better' school. It is only when the graph goes off the chart that we need to start to worry, because then things get less predictable and less manageable. Incremental change suddenly becomes discontinuous change. Catastrophe theory, they call it in mathematics, interestingly and symbolically, the study of discontinuous curves in observed phenomena, graphs that loop back on themselves or go into precipitous falls or unsuspected plateaux. Trends, after all, cannot accelerate forever on a graph paper without looping the loop.

I believe that discontinuity is not catastrophe, and that it certainly *need* not be catastrophe. Indeed, I will argue that discontinuous change is the only way forward for a tramlined society, one that has got used to its ruts and its blinkers and prefers its own ways, however dreary, to untrodden paths and new ways of looking at things. I like the story of the Peruvian Indians who, seeing the sails of their Spanish invaders on the horizon put it down to a freak of the weather and went on about their business, having no concept of sailing ships in their limited experience. Assuming continuity, they screened out what did not fit and let disaster in. I like less the story that a frog if put in cold water will not bestir itself if that water is heated up slowly and gradually and will in the end let itself be boiled alive, too comfortable with continuity to realize that continuous change at some point becomes discontinous and demands a change in behaviour. If we want to avoid the fate of the Peruvian Indians or the boiling frog we must learn to look for and embrace discontinuous change.

That is more revolutionary than it sounds. Discontinous, after all, is hardly a word to stir the multitudes; yet to embrace discontinous change means, for instance, completely re-thinking the way in which we learn things. In a world of incremental change it is sensible to ape your elders in order to take over where they leave off, in both knowledge and responsibility. But under conditions of discontinuity it is no longer obvious that their ways should continue to be your ways; we may all need new rules for new ball games and will have to discover them for ourselves. Learning then becomes the voyage of exploration, of questing and experimenting, that scientists and tiny children know it to be but which we are soon reminded, by parents, teachers and supervisors, can be time-wasting when others already know what we need to learn. It is a way of learning which can even be seen as disrespectful if not downright rebellious. Assume discontinuity in our affairs, in other words, and you threaten the authority of the holders of knowledge, of those in charge or those in power.

For those in charge continuity is comfort, and predictability ensures that they can continue in control. Instinctively, therefore, they prefer to believe that things will go on as they have before. It requires, as Mancur Olsen has argued, revolutions to unblock societies and shocks to galvanize organizations. Perhaps that is why Britain, untouched by revolution for over 300 years, seems to prefer that the status quo should be the way forward and why organizations too often learn too late.

Major change in organizations seems to follow a predictable and sad sequence:

FRIGHT	– the possibility of bankruptcy, takeover or collapse
NEW FACES	– new people are brought in at the top
NEW QUESTIONS	– questions, study groups, investigations into old ways and new options
NEW STRUCTURES	– the existing pattern is broken up and re-arranged to give new talent scope and break up old clubs
NEW GOALS & STANDARDS	– the new organization sets itself new aims and targets.

Do we always need a painful jolt to start re-thinking? Did it need the Titanic to sink before it became compulsory for ships to carry enough lifeboats for all the passengers? Did the Challenger shuttle have to explode before NASA re-organized its decision-making systems and priorities?

How many have to die before we make cars safer and less powerful?

It is the argument of this book that discontinuous change is all around us. We would be foolish to block our eyes to its signs as those Peruvian Indians did to their invaders' sails. We need not leave it too late, like the frog in boiling water, nor wait for a revolution. There are opportunities as well as problems in discontinuous change. If we change our attitudes, our habits and the ways of some of our institutions it can be an age of new discovery, new enlightenment and new freedoms, an age of true learning.

Ask people, as I have often done, to recall two or three of the most important learning experiences in their lives and they will never tell you of courses taken or degrees obtained, but of brushes with death, of crises encountered, of new and unexpected challenges or confrontations. They will tell you, in other words, of times when continuity ran out on them, when they had no past experience to fall back on, no rules or handbook. They survived, however, and came to count it as learning, as a growth experience. Discontinuous change, therefore, when properly handled, is the way we grow up.

The Beginnings Are Small

We live life on two levels. A teenager in the USA was asked to produce a list of the kinds of critical events which she saw looming in the future. It went like this:

A US/USSR alliance
A cancer cure
Test-tube babies
An accidental nuclear explosion
Spread of anarchy throughout the world
Robots holding political office in the USA

We could each provide our own such list of triumphs and disasters. When she was asked, however, to list the critical events looming in her personal life she wrote down:

Moving into my own apartment
Interior Design School
Driver's Licence
Getting a dog
Marriage
Having Children
Death

This book is about changes, but it is about the changes which will affect the *second* list more than the first. Not that a cancer cure or a nuclear war would not have an effect on the way we live our daily lives, but such mega changes belong to other books by other people. This book is written in the belief that it is often the little things in life which change things most and last the longest.

The chimney, for instance, may have caused more social change than any war. Without a chimney everyone had to huddle together in one central place around a fire with a hole in the roof above. The chimney, with its separate flues, made it possible for one dwelling to heat a variety of rooms. Small units could huddle together independently. The cohesion of the tribe in winter slipped away.

Central heating – meaning in reality decentralized heating – carried it even further, doing away with fireplaces altogether, making it possible to pile dwelling units on top of dwelling units into the sky and for so many people to live alone, often far above the ground, but warm.

No one would want to disinvent the chimney or central heating, but their inventors (whose names are long lost if they were ever known) could not have guessed at the changes which they would make to our social architecture. I shall argue in this book, amongst other things, that the telephone line has been and will be the modern day equivalent of the chimney, unintentionally changing the way we work and live.

I saw a man sitting in his car in the parking place I coveted. 'Are you about to move?' I asked. 'Not for a couple of hours yet,' he replied. It was then I saw the portable computer on the seat beside him and the fax connected to his car telephone line. He was using his car as a mobile office.

Rather like central heating, the telephone and its attachments make it possible today for people to work together without being together in one place. The scattered organization is now a reality. The implications, as we shall see, are considerable. It is not an unmixed blessing for being together has always been part of the fun. As Pascal once said, all the world's ills stem from the fact that a man cannot sit in a room alone. Increasingly, he, and she, may have to.

Chimneys and telephones are technology – always a

potential trigger of discontinuity. Economic reality is another. Governments can stave it off for a while but not forever. In the end countries live or die according to their comparative advantage. Comparative advantage means that there is something for which others will pay a price, be it oil and minerals, cheap labour, golden sun or brains. For Britain and the rest of the industrialized world it has, increasingly, to be brains. Clever people, making clever things or providing clever services add value, sometimes lots of value, to minimal amounts of raw material. Their sales allow the import of all the things we cannot grow and cannot afford to make. That way prosperity advances. It sounds straightforward and simple enough, but its consequences ramble everywhere. Many more clever people are now needed, for one thing, with fewer places for the less clever. Organizations making or doing clever things spend much of their time handling information in all sorts of forms. Facts, figures, words, pictures, ideas, arguments, meetings, committees, papers, conferences all proliferate. Information goes down telephone lines, so technology and economics begin to blend together to create a massive discontinuity in the shape, and skills and purposes of many of our organizations. Clever organizations do not, it seems, work the way organizations used to work, they have different shapes, different working habits, different age profiles, different traditions of authority.

Barry Jones, now an Australian Cabinet Minister, has listed the typical activities of the information sector.

teaching	creative arts & architecture
research	design
office work	music
public service	data processing
communications	computer software
the media	selling
films	accountancy

theatre	law
photography	psychiatry & psychology
post & telecommunications	social work
book publishing	management
printing	advertising
banking	church
real estate	science
administration	trade unions
museums & television	parliament

One could add to it: stockbroking, consultancy, journalism, conference organizing, secretarial work, medicine, politics and local government.

It is unlikely that anyone reading this book will not find his or her work included in this list.

Technology and economics is a potent blend. It is the premise of this book that from that blend all sorts of changes ensue. Social customs can be transformed. An information society makes it easier for more women to do satisfying jobs. Technology has turned child-bearing into an act of positive decision for most. Marriage then becomes, increasingly, a public commitment to starting a family. Relationships that do not involve the start of a family no longer need the stamp of public commitment. Women can support themselves and can in theory support a family on their own, and many will prefer to do just that. What was in former times technologically and economically impossible, and therefore socially unacceptable, becomes both possible and acceptable. Discontinuity abroad creeps unnoticed into the family.

Words are the bugles of social change. When our language changes, behaviour will not be far behind. House-husbands, single-parent families, 'dinkies' and 'telecom-muters', these and many other words were unknown ten years ago. They were not needed. Organizations used to invite men to bring their wives to functions, then it became 'spouses' in recognition of the growing number of female employees, then 'partners' as an acceptance that marriage is not the only stable relationship, and now in California it is the 'significant other' to take care of any conceivable situation.

Just Think Of It!

It is the combination of a changing technology and economics, in particular of information technology and biotechnology and the economics associated with them, which causes this discontinuity. Between them they will make the world a different place.

Information technology links the processing power of the computer with the microwaves, the satellites, and the fibre optic cables of telecommunications. It is a technology which is leaping rather than creeping into the future. It is said that if the automobile industry had developed as rapidly as the processing capacity of the computer we would now be able to buy a 400 mile-per-gallon Rolls-Royce for £1.

Biotechnology is the completely new industry that has grown out of the interpretation of DNA, the genetic code at the heart of life. It is only one generation old as a science and as an industry, and is only now becoming evident in everyday life with new types of crops, genetic fingerprinting and all the possibilities, good and bad, of what is called bio-engineering.

These two technologies are developing so fast that their outputs are unpredictable, but some of the more likely developments in the next ten to twenty years could change parts of our lives, and other peoples' lives, in a dramatic fashion. A group of young executives who were asked by their companies to contemplate 2000 AD came up with the following possibilities and probabilities.

Cordless telephones Mark 2

The next generation of cordless telephones may give everyone their own portable personal telephone to be used anywhere at affordable prices. Link it to a lap-top computer and a portable fax and a car or train seat becomes an office. More interestingly, a telephone will then belong to a person not to a place. We will call a person and not know where they are.

Monoclonal antibodies

These genetically engineered bacteria which work to prevent particular diseases already exist and will be expanded. Blood-clotting and anti-clotting agents can now be manufactured to prevent major coronary diseases. 'Scavenger Proteins' are under investigation, designed to locate undesirable substances in the bloodstream, such as excess cholesterol. Cures for most cancers, and possibly AIDS, will be available by the end of the century. Senile dementia is now understood and drugs to combat it are under development. Life could go on, if not forever, for a lot longer than before when most diseases can be cured or prevented.

The transgenic pig

The possibility of using animal organs in humans has been under investigation for some time. The pig is biologically similar to humans and experiments are under way to engineer embryos to produce the transgenic pig, an animal with organs more man-like than piglike. Pig farms may one day mean something quite different from what they do today and replacement organs could be available on demand.

Water fields

Crops can now be genetically engineered to grow on poor quality soil or even in water (without tasting like seaweed!). Under development is an idea to engineer crops which can take their nitrogen directly from the air instead of from the ground, reducing the need for fertilizer. Any country could one day grow all the food it needs.

Enzyme catalysts

Microbes can now be used as catalysts in many chemical manufacturing processes. Some microbes can even be used to extract minerals from low-grade areas which were previously uneconomic. There are bugs which can be trained to devour and break down waste materials and can even thrive on cyanide. Rubbish disposal is now part of the chemical industry. Indeed, waste can now be converted into methane as one contribution to the energy problem. We shall see, too, self-cleaning ships which will biologically repel barnacles from sticking to their hulls.

Expert G.P.s

Computers programmed with up-to-date medical knowledge will be available to all doctors. These medical expert systems will not replace the doctor but will allow every doctor to be a better doctor, to make fewer demands on specialists and so release them to be better specialists. This example of 'expert systems' to enhance the work of professionals and technicians will be copied in all types of occupations, from the solicitor's office to the supermarket purchasing department.

The hearing computer

Voice-sensitive computers which can translate the spoken word into written words on a screen will be on every executive's desk one day, turning everyone into their own typist whether they can use a keyboard or not.

Irradiated food

Irradiation, once we are convinced that it is safe, will make it possible to buy 'fresh' food from all round the world at any time of the year. There will also be appetite-reducing drugs for those who find the new foods too tempting, and even health-increasing foods for those who want it both ways.

Telecatalogues
Teleshopping, already in existence in experimental situations, will one day be commonplace. Every store will display its wares and prices on your home television teletext, with local pick-up centres available for those unwilling to pay the extra delivery charge. Personal shopping in the High Street will become a leisure activity rather than a necessity, with all the frills and fancies that go with something done for pleasure not for duty.

Smart cards
These cards, already in use in France, replace cash, keys, credit, debit and cash cards. They will not only let you into your home or your car but will automatically update all your bank account balances for you.

Genetic fingerprints
Instead of Personal Identification Numbers (PINs) which are easy to discover and replicate, we shall each have a fingerprint on our personal cards which cannot be reproduced by others.

Genetic fingerprinting can be used to detect criminals from remains of tissue left behind at the scene of a crime, and also to diagnose hereditary and latent diseases. A national data-bank of genetic fingerprints seems possible one day.

Soon, everything we know about ourselves, and somethings we do not know, will be available to anyone with the right number or fingerprint. What price privacy then, many will ask.

Windscreen Maps
Computerized autoguidance screens will become common-

place, telling you the best way to get to where you want to go and projected onto the windscreen, as in fighter aircraft, so that you need not take your eyes off the road. These systems can take weather, traffic density and roadworks into account and give you the best available route, turning the whole country, one suspects, into a constant traffic jam.

Mileage bills

Cables laid under the roads of our cities can trigger a meter inside a car programmed to charge different parts of the city at different rates, presenting you with the equivalent of a telephone bill at the end of the month for the use of your car on the city roads. Already designed for Hong Kong this system is potentially available now, although special licences for inner-city use are a more likely first step.

The technology we shall undoubtedly take in our stride. Hole-in-the-wall banking caused hardly a flutter of an eyelid when it appeared and video-recorders are now part of the furniture in many homes. It is not the technology itself that is important but the impact which, without conscious thought, it has on our lives. Microwave ovens were a clever idea, but their inventor could hardly have realized that the effect, once they were everywhere, would be to take the preparation of food out of the home and into the, increasingly automated, factory; to make cooking as it used to be into an activity of choice, not of necessity; to alter the habits of our homes, making the dining table outmoded for many, as each member of the family individually heats up his or her own meal as and when they require it; 'grazing', the advertising people call it.

Whether these developments are for good or for ill must be our choice. Technology in itself is neutral. We can use it to enrich our lives or to let them lose all meaning. What we cannot do is to pretend that nothing has changed and live in a garden of remembrance as if time had stood still. It doesn't and we can't.

Thinking Upside-Down

Discontinuous change requires discontinuous thinking. If the new way of things is going to be different from the old, not just an improvement on it, then we shall need to look at everything in a new way. The new words really will signal new ideas. Not unnaturally, discontinuous upside-down thinking has never been popular with the upholders of continuity and the status quo. Copernicus and Galileo, arch-exponents of upside-down thinking, were not thanked for their pains. Jesus Christ, with his teaching that the meek should inherit the earth, that the poor were blessed and the first should be last in the ultimate scheme of things, died an untimely and unpleasant death. Nonetheless, their ideas live on, as good ideas do, to release new energies and new possibilities. In the long perspective of history it may seem that the really influential people in the last 100 years were not Hitler or Churchill, Stalin or Gorbachev, but Freud, Marx and Einstein, men who changed nothing except the way we think, but that changed everything. Francis Crick is not today a household name, yet he, with James Watson and Maurice Wilkins, discovered the genetic code, DNA, and so created the science of microbiology and the industry of biotechnology on which much of our economic future may depend.

The creative upside-down thinking of such people is the premise on which this book is built. New ways of thinking about familiar things can release new energies and make all manner of things possible. Upside-down thinking does not have to aspire to the greatness of Einstein or the all-embracing doctrines of Marx. It has its more familiar variants. The person who decides to treat every chore as an opportunity for learning discovers that cooking can be a creative art, chopping wood a craft, childminding an educational experience and shopping a sociological expedition. The organization which treats people like assets, requiring maintenance, love and investment, can behave quite differently from the organization which looks upon them as costs, to be reduced wherever and whenever possible. Upside-down thinking changes nothing save the way we think, but that can make all the difference.

This book advocates shamrocks, doughnuts and portfolios. These new words are not intended to be humorous devices but to evoke new images of familiar things. Thirty years ago Donald Schon, an American writer on organizations and now on learning, was arguing that creativity, particularly scientific creativity, comes from the 'displacement of concepts' – from taking concepts from one field of life and applying them to another in order to bring fresh insights. Einstein's Theory of Relativity is the great example. It applies equally well, if not more so, to the field of human activities. New imagery, signalled by new words, is as important as new theory; indeed new theory without new imagery can go unnoticed. Most of what is in this book is not new, nor is it being said for the first time, but much of it has gone unnoticed.

Upside-down thinking invites one to consider the unlikely if not the absurd. If Copernicus could stand the solar system on its head and still be right nothing should be dismissed out of hand in a time of discontinuity.

— Upside-down thinking suggests that we should stop talking and thinking of employees and employment. They are words, after all, which only entered the English language some 100 years ago. If work were defined as activity, some of which is paid for, then everyone is a worker, for nearly all their natural life. If everyone were treated as self-employed during their active years then by law and logic they could not be *un*employed. They might be poor but that can be put right. The words 'retirement' and 'unemployment' used only as a contrast to 'employment' would cease to be useful.

— Upside-down thinking suggests that if we put *everyone* on welfare it would no longer be invidious to receive it. That would not mean that no one was expected to work, only that everyone, as of right, got an initial 'social dividend', to be repaid progressively as one earns.

— Upside down thinking wonders what magic it is that determines that forty hours spread over five days should be the working week for most people. Why cannot one choose to distribute the 2000 hours per year of normal work in a wide variety of chunks?

— Upside-down thinking notices that marriages in the last century lasted fifteen years and today also for fifteen years. In the last century it was the death of a partner which ended the marriage, now it is divorce. Should all relationships as well as employment contracts have a fixed term?

— Upside-down thinking suggests that it might be desirable to reward some experts for *not* using their skills. At present dentists are paid per treatment. There is an inevitable temptation to diagnose the need for treatment. If rewards were related to the number of healthy mouths in the practise not the bad ones, we might need fewer dentists and have better teeth. Similarly, upside-down thinking observes that a national health service is run and rewarded as a national sickness service and wonders why it cannot be reversed.

— Upside-down thinking suggests that instead of a *National* Curriculum for education what is really needed is an *individual* curriculum for every child, within common guidelines maybe, but given expression in a formal contract between the home and the school.

— Upside-down thinking questions whether more money

for more effort is always the right way to reward all the people all the time, or whether at certain stages in life more time might be as welcome as more money.

— Upside-down thinking wonders why one career or one type of job should be the norm. Why not three careers, switching progressively from energy to wisdom as the years role on?

— Upside-down thinking wonders why assistants are always younger than their principals or superiors. Why could not people retrain in mid-life to be part-time assistants to doctors, teachers, social workers and lawyers, para-professionals leaving the full professionals to do the more specialized work.

— Upside-down thinking wonders why roads are free and railways expensive in most countries, and suspects that it ought to be the other way around, as it almost is in Italy.

— In organizations, upside-down thinking observes that authority now has to be earned from those people over whom it is exercised and that even formal appraisal systems are upside-down in some organizations these days, with the subordinates appraising their bosses.

— Upside-down thinking notes that before too long there will be more people working outside organizations than inside them and that, even now, organizations only employ, directly, about one-quarter of the people connected in some way with the product or service which they deliver.

— Upside-down thinking suggests, therefore, that it might be better to pay people for the work they do, not the time they spend, since that time cannot be measured if they are out of sight or out of the organization.

And so it can go on. At first sight impossible, or ludicrous, many of these ideas have already been canvased as practical possibilities in some quarters. This book will consider some of them in the wake of the changes thrown up by the new discontinuities in work.

It is a time for new imaginings, of windows opening even if some doors close. We need not stumble backwards into the future, casting longing glances at what used to be; we can turn round and face a changed reality. It is, after all, a safer posture if you want to keep moving.

Some people, however, do not want to keep moving. Change for them means sacrificing the familiar, even if it is unpleasant, for the unknown, even when it might be better. Better the hole they know rather than the one not yet dug. Sadly for them a time of discontinuous change means that standing still is not an option, for the ground is shifting underneath them. For them, more than for the movers and the shakers, it is essential that they understand what is happening, that they begin to appreciate that to move and to change is essential, and that through change we learn and grow, although not always without pain.

This book is written particularly for those who live in the midst of change and do not notice it or want it. It is not a textbook for would-be leaders, nor a political tract; more a guidebook to a new country, ending with some tips for the traveller.

It is, however, only one man's view. In an age of unreason there can be no certainty. The guidebook is a guide to a country in which few have yet travelled, a country still to be explored. It is not my purpose to convince anyone that all forecasts are inevitable or that all my prescriptions are right. Rather I am concerned to persuade people that the world around them is indeed changing, with consequences yet to be understood. An age of unreason is an age of opportunity even if it looks at first sight more like the end of all ages.

If this book helps at all to look at things in a different way, if it sometimes creates an 'Aha' effect, as when people say 'Aha, of course, that is the way it is,' if people start to think 'unreasonably' and try to shape their world the way they think it ought to be, then I shall be content.

2 The Numbers

The numbers are the key. They explain why things will not continue as they were because they have already gone beyond the point of no return. It is just that most of us have not noticed. The numbers are the numbers of people, the numbers working, numbers dying, numbers growing up. Demography is a boring word for a mesmerizing subject.

The New Minority

Less than half of the workforce in the industrialized world will be in 'proper' full-time jobs in organizations by the beginning of the 21st century. Those full-timers or insiders will be the new minority, just when we had begun to think that proper jobs were the norm for everyone. The others will not be all unemployed, although in every country there will be some who belong to this 'reserve army' as Marx called it. More will be self-employed, more and more every year; many will be part-timers or temporary workers, sometimes because that is the way they want it, sometimes because that is all that is on offer. And then there is, everywhere, another reserve army of women in waiting, those whom the OECD so accurately calls 'unpaid domestic workers', mothers whose talents and energies are not totally absorbed by their families. Add all these disparate groups together and *already* they just about equal the numbers of those with the full-time proper jobs.

When less than half the available workforce is in full-time employment it no longer makes sense to think of a full-time job as the norm. Continuous change will have flipped into discontinuous change and we shall begin to change our views of 'work', of 'the job' and of 'a career'.

The reason for the shift is the emergence of the shamrock organization. The shamrock organization is explained in Chapter 3. Essentially, it is a form of organization based around a core of essential executives and workers supported by outside contractors and part-time help. This is not a new way of organizing things builders large and small have operated this way for generations, as have newspapers with their printers and their stringers, or farmers with contract harvesting and holiday labour. What is new is the growth of this way of organizing in the big businesses and in the institutions of the public sector. All organizations will soon be shamrock organizations.

It has grown because it is cheaper. Organizations have realized that while it may be convenient to have everyone around all the time, with their time at your command because you have bought all their time, it is a luxurious way of marshalling the necessary resources. It is cheaper to keep them outside the organization, employed by themselves or by specialist contractors, and to buy their services when you need them.

This is a sensible strategy when labour is plentiful, when you can pick and choose between suppliers. It is a sensible strategy when your work ebbs and flows as it tends to do in service industries. When you are manufacturing things any surplus resources of people or equipment can always be turned to good advantage by producing things for stock for the weeks of peak demand, but the *service* industries cannot, or at least should not, stockpile their customers and must therefore flex their workforce.

Both these factors currently exist. The labour supply, the potential workforce, is growing in all the industrialized countries as the boom babies of the 1960s, and their wives, join the workforce during the 1990s – an extra million or so in Britain, for instance. At the same time the shift to the service sector continues inexorably everywhere. Between 1960 and 1985 the share of employees in the service sector in the USA rose from 56 to 69 per cent and in Italy from 33 to 55 per cent. It is unlikely to change back. The two factors work on each other; a growing service sector offers greater opportunities to women, which increases the potential workforce, which in turn increases the potential for more flexible ways of organizing.

It has been happening slowly, so slowly that most people have not noticed the new dimensions. Like the frog in Chapter 1, the temperature changes so gradually that no reaction is called for – until it is, perhaps, too late. Before very long the full-time worker will be a minority of the working population. Our assumptions about how the world works, how taxes are collected, families supported, lives planned and corporations organized will have to change radically. The Universal Declaration of Human Rights, which in 1947 guaranteed a choice of job to everyone, will be a clear anachronism. The new minority signals a major discontinuity which will effect every family in every industrialized country within the next generation.

The New Intelligentsia

The second number is alarming in a different way. A study by McKinsey's Amsterdam office in 1986 estimated that 70 per cent of all jobs in Europe in the year 2000 would require cerebral skills rather than manual skills. In the USA the figure is expected to be 80 per cent. That would be a complete reversal of the world of work some fifty years earlier. Discontinuity indeed!

It is impossible to be precise about such things. There is, to start with, no clearcut distinction between a cerebral job, requiring brain skills, and a manual job, needing muscles. Even simple manual jobs, like gardening, now need a degree of brains to understand the proper use of fertilizers and herbicides, to distinguish plant varieties and maintain machinery. Nonetheless, looking back at the list of occupations in the information sector on pages 12–13, a sector where brain skills of some degree are essential, it is hard not to think that 70 per cent is, if anything, an undercstimate.

What is more controversial and even more alarming is the estimate by McKinsey's that one half of these brain-skill jobs will require the equivalent of a higher education, or a professional qualification, to be done adequately. If that is even approximately true it means that some 35 per cent of an age group should today be entering higher education or its equivalent if the labour force is going to be adequately skilled by the year 2000. McKinsey's estimate may even be on the conservative side. If we look at the new jobs alone, the current expectation is that 60 per cent of them will be managerial or professional, graduates all, of some sort.

In spite of these trends the percentage of young people in Britain going on to higher education is currently 14 per cent, rising to 18 per cent by 1992, but only because there will be fewer teenagers in total. In the rest of Europe the overall figure is around 20 per cent, with small national differences. In France, for instance, 36 per cent pass their *baccalauréat* and are therefore entitled to enter university but nearly half leave, or are asked to leave, at the end of the first year. Only Japan, the USA, Taiwan and South Korea seem to have university populations of the right sort of size for the future, and in all these countries there are concerns about the quality if not the quantity of some of what is called higher education.

If these estimates of the required levels of education are even partly true it means that not only will we see alarming numbers of skill shortages but that, more seriously still, we may lack the skills and the wits even to create the businesses and the opportunities which will then encounter skill shortages! It will, of course, be an invisible discontinuity. We will not miss the organizations we have not had, and never thought to have. Like the frog in Chapter 1 it will just be a slow unnoticed death.

The Vanishing Generation

In the nineties there will be almost one quarter fewer young people leaving school. At first glance this seems like a timely end to the problem of youth unemployment. A second glance changes the picture because it points to even more pressure on the relatively small percentage who have the brain skills needed by today's workforce. The bulk of the new reduced cohort of young people will still be like those, 43 per cent of them in 1986, who leave British schools without a proper certificate in even one subject.

A 1988 British Report by the National Economic Development Office and the Training Commission, 'Young People and the Labour Market, A Challenge for the 1990s', pointed out that in 1987 less than twenty large employers took on half of all the 27,000 school leavers with two or more A-levels who were looking for work. The vanishing generation, therefore, is a problem because, if nothing is done, it means that the supply of brain skills, already inadequate, will be even more inadequate, and that the skills shortages referred to above will become even more severe. The competition for the more educated will intensify and the rejection of the less educated will be felt even more cruelly. Youth unemployment will *not* be solved, indeed it will be raised a notch or two.

The situation is an opportunity, however, if it makes it easier to tackle the task of educating more of our young men and women for life and work in the world of brain skills. Without doing anything, as every government has discovered, the *percentages* of those going on to higher and further education are bound to improve as the base number falls. Doing rather more will, in percentage terms, make a deal of difference and will set markers for the future.

Those markers are important because they must change a culture. There is no innate reason why Britain should be sixteenth in the OECD league table of young people in education after 16 years of age – above only Portugal and Spain. British teenagers are not innately more stupid or less educable; they are the inheritors of a tradition which held that book learning was for the few, that real life, and real money, should begin as soon as possible and that manual and pragmatic skills were best learnt on the job. The past, as so often in Europe, determines the future although, however true these beliefs might have been in the world of work as it used to be, they must be less true today.

In Japan, top of the OECD table, 98 per cent of young people stay on in formal education until 18 years of age even though that education is far from stimulating and far from being pragmatic. They are the inheritors of a different cultural tradition, one that just happens to be more attuned to the needs of the future than that of Britain and most of the rest of Europe. In America, too, the young stay on in school, but whether they learn anything there is a question of growing concern.

The information society, after all, uses information, be it in the form of numbers, words, pictures or voices, on screens, in books or in printouts and reports, as its currency. The essential requirement, therefore, of all its workers is that they are able to read, interpret and fit together the elements of this currency, irrespective, almost, of what the data actually relates to. That is a skill of the brain. It can be taught or at least developed in classrooms. It does not, for most people, happen quickly, easily or early but requires years of practice, years which are most conveniently and usefully spent at the beginning of adult life rather than inconveniently in the middle. This general skill is akin to riding a bicycle, once learnt it is never unlearnt, and having learnt it one can then go on to learn its use in particular applications.

It is this conviction that brain skills are of general use and can be developed in youth that has led places like Taiwan and South Korea, following Japan, to put such an emphasis on the formal, even scholastic, education of their youth. It has been said that every second person in Seoul has either been at university or is currently studying or teaching there, while in the 1970s Mr Goh Thock Tong, then Minister for Trade and Industry in Singapore, was arguing that Singapore needed 'to step into the shoes left behind by countries like Germany and Japan as they restructure, they from skill-intensive to knowledge-intensive and we from labour-intensive to skill-intensive'. In pursuit of these objectives Singapore proceeded to increase greatly the number of university places and lower the entry requirements. Britain, who needs to be one step ahead of Singapore, has until recently been doing the reverse.

The opportunity, however, remains and is made easier by the vanishing generation. The statistic is also good news for those who want to re-enter or enter late the work of the information society. The squeeze on qualified youth will encourage employers to turn to other sources of skill, particularly to women, many of whom have the necessary early education but have been busy working to raise their families and manage their homes. Less convenient as employees because they want and need more flexibility, they have not been wooed too assiduously in the past. In the 1990s they will be. They do, after all, represent nearly half of all university entrants (over half in 1987 in the USA for the first time). They are a neglected resource which few will be able to neglect once the vanishing generation begins to bite. The NEDO Report cited above estimates that four out of five of the 900,000 extra workers it foresees in Britain's workforce over the next eight years will be women returning to work.

Women have re-entered the workforce before, but the numbers and the conditions which they will expect in the 1990s turn this into a significant discontinuity which will change the way organizations are run, will affect family structures and living patterns quite significantly – all issues to be explored in subsequent chapters.

The Third Age

In 1988 the Social Affairs Ministers of the OECD met to contemplate the time when one person in five will be a pensioner and one in ten aged over 75, when there will be only three people of working age to support each pensioner and when old-age pensions may account for one-fifth of national income. It will be even worse for Switzerland and West Germany where there will be only two people of working age for each old person.

It will be 2040 before this scenario fully becomes a reality, but the people who will be old then are alive now and unless they quickly change their breeding habits the numbers of their children are quite predictable. This world will happen and it will start to happen before the end of this century.

Once again, there have been old people before, but never before so many of them. I knew only one grandparent – the others had died before I was born. My children knew all four. Their children will almost certainly know a great-grandparent or two. People in their sixties and retired will still be someone's children. The infrequent has become the commonplace and the world as we know it will inevitably change in some way.

- It is happening because, in the richer countries, it is becoming harder to die. Each major cause of death is either diminished, like smallpox or polio and, one day, cancer, or postponed for a few more years or decades, like heart disease. Of course, nature, or man's tampering with nature, may trigger another plague and some wonder whether AIDS may not be just that plague, but such disasters excepted there seems little reason why many of today's teenagers cannot expect to live to 100, provided they do not drink, smoke or drive themselves to death.

The question is, will they want to live that long? When death as an act of God seems to be indefinitely postponed will we want to make it increasingly an act of mankind? Euthanasia, already quasi-legal in the Netherlands, may become more acceptable to more societies.

More urgent are the questions 'What will they live on?' 'What will they do?' 'Who will care for them?' By the year 2020, if nothing changes, Italy will be spending over a quarter of her national income on pensions, while Britain's health service spends ten times as much on a patient over 75 as on one of working age.

Like all discontinuities, however, this one contains opportunities as well as problems if the changes are seen coming and if everyone concerned can indulge in a little upside-down thinking.

They will not all be poor, for instance. An increasing number of them will own their own homes, an asset which can be turned into an annual income provided that they do not intend to bequeath it to the next generation (who will by then be in mid or late career with their own homes bought and paid for). Most of them will be healthy and active. That is, of course, why they are still alive. They are capable of working. One British study found that 43 per cent of over-65s regularly helped other elderly people, 25 per cent helped the disabled, 11 per cent helped neighbours. If we change our view of work to include such unpaid activity then these people are only retired in a legal or technical sense. After all, in the last century no one had heard of retirement – they worked till they dropped, or, as a farmer said once when I asked him what was the difference between farming at 75 and farming at 50, 'The same only slower!' Experience and wisdom can often compensate for energy.

So many older people will not go unnoticed, particularly when many more of them will have experienced responsibility earlier in life and will not be used to keeping quiet. If we are sensible we will want to use their talents in our organizations, but not full-time or on full pay. We shall need, then, to re-think what jobs call for part-time wisdom and experience and what work can be done at a distance by responsible people. We shall need to revise the tax rules for pensions to make it economic for such work to be done. Many people, active and healthy, will devise their own activities, organizing around their enthusiasms; we must not let too many rules from the past stand in their way. We will need to change the way we talk about them, words like 'retirement' will become as redundant as 'servant' today. Words are so often the heralds of social change, the outward signs of a discontinuity at work triggering some upside-down thinking.

Already the linguistic signposts are going up. The Third Age, the age of living, as the French would have it, which follows the first age of learning and the second of working, is already becoming a common term. There is a University of the Third Age, a network of people exchanging their skills and their knowledge. There will soon be more talk of Third Age Careers. Soon, no doubt, there will be Third Age societies and, ultimately, Ministers for the Third Age in all OECD countries! The wrinklies, as my children fondly term us, can be assets as well as liabilities, *if* we want them to be.

If words are indeed the heralds of change, then the Third Age language suggests that before too long we shall be referring to people's job-careers as we now do to their education. 'Where did you work?' for a 65-year-old with fifteen years, at least, of life ahead will sound much like 'Where did you go to school?' It would all sound strange indeed to my father who died two years after retiring, at the age of 74. For him there was no Third Age worth living and the second age, of job and career, had long been a burden before he could afford to leave it.

It will be different for us, his children, and for our children. It is change of a discontinuous sort, but it need not be change for the worse if we can see it coming and can prepare for it.

$$\frac{100,000}{2} \, (4) = J$$

The changes which are coming to our ways of work and living, indeed the changes which are already here, are conveniently summed up by this strange equation. When it is unravelled, it will suggest that we have, for some time now, been engaged in a massive job-splitting exercise in our society and have not even noticed it.

It will work like this. Thirty years ago when I joined an international company and started my job I signed on, although I never realized it, for 100,000 hours of work during my lifetime, because I should, if I was anything like everyone else in the developed world at that time, be expected to work for 47 hours a week, including overtime paid or unpaid, for 47 weeks a year for 47 years of my life (from, on average, 18 to 65). $47 \times 47 \times 47 = 103,823$ or $100,000$ hours give or take a few.

My teenage son and daughter, a generation later, can

expect their *jobs* to add up, on average, to 50, 000 hours. The lifetime job will have been halved in one generation. At first sight this would imply that they would be working half as many hours per week, for half as many weeks and half as many years. But mathematics does not work like that. Just as half of 4^3 (64) is not 2^3 (8), so half of 47^3 is not 23.5^3. In fact, rather bizarrely, half of the three 47s is three 37s, for $37 \times 37 \times 37 = 50, 653$.

It is because of this statistical sleight-of-hand that we have not noticed this rather dramatic piece of discontinuous change. It is also, in part, because it is only now beginning to bite as the next generation begin their second age of jobs and careers.

The world is not so neat, however, as to switch uniformly from the three 47s to the three 37s. That is where the (4) comes in. My daughter and my son have four principal options to choose from.

In the first option they will follow in their father's footsteps and look for a full-time job, or at least a sequence of full-time jobs, in the core of an organization or perhaps as a professional of some sort. In this case their working week will not be that different from the one I knew. Statistically it will average 45 hours per week, with rather less overtime for the hourly paid and fewer Saturday mornings for office workers. Nor will their working year be much reduced; longer annual holidays bring it down to 45 weeks rather than 47.

What will change, however, is the length of their job life. To get one of those increasingly rare jobs in the core or the professions (less than half of all jobs by 2000) they will need to be both well-qualified *and* experienced. In Germany today, a six- or seven-year university course is piled on top of eighteen months of military or community service so that the average entrant into the job market is 27 years of age. In the USA, a postgraduate qualification of some sort, after a four-year degree, is increasingly becoming a prerequisite of a good job, making 24 the normal starting age in a proper job. Britain still has three-year degree courses (except in Scotland) and no military service, but employers increasingly look for further qualifications of a more vocational or professional nature *and* for relevant experience in vacations or 'gap' years. It has, after all, been the established practice in the older professions of medicine, architecture and the law for centuries – a long (seven-year) mix of education, experience and vocational training. We can expect to see it extend to many other occupations, with the result that British parents must increasingly expect to wait until the offspring are 24 or 25 before they are established in a full-time job, if that is what they want.

It is possible that the fall in the numbers of qualified young people in all industrialized countries will tempt organizations and professions to shorten their training requirements in order to get the best of a reducing supply. The form this will probably take, however, will be to finance them, perhaps under the guise of employment, during their studies. It will be education more generously funded, not a job.

The next generation of full-time core workers, therefore, be they professionals, managers, technicians or skilled workers, can expect to start their full-time careers later – and to leave them earlier. This is the crucial point. The core worker will have a harder but shorter job, with more people leaving full-time employment in their late forties or early fifties, partly because they no longer want the pressure that such jobs will increasingly entail, but mainly because there will be younger more qualified and more energetic people available for these core jobs.

It is true that early in the next century the total number of people in the workforce in every country will start to decline and the average age to rise, as the dip in the birthrate of the 1970s works its way through life, but the reducing numbers of the full-timers will continue to place a premium on youth, energy and qualifications whenever they can get them in combination. It will be a shorter life but a more furious one for the full-timers, as the new professionals in business are already discovering.

The nett result of these changes will be a full-time job which, on average, will result in 45 hours for 45 weeks for 25 years, totalling 50,000 hours. Work won't stop for such people after 50 but it will not be the same sort of work; it will not be a *job* as they have known it. They will enter their Third Age sooner than others, affluent, no doubt, but still with a good third of their lives to live.

It is happening already. One personnel manager was surprised to discover that only 2 per cent of his workforce were, as he put it, still there at the official retirement age of 62. What he had done was to look back fifteen years to all those who were then 47 and had found that only a few had stayed on with the organization for the remaining fifteen years. Some had moved to new jobs and one or two had died, but the great majority had opted for, or been persuaded into, early retirement in their fifties. 'We knew that people were leaving us early,' he said, 'but we had no idea of the scale of it all until we started counting.' An advertising agency, aware that creativity and mental energy tend to decline with the years, would like to see everyone under the age of 50. They have not, so far, been allowed by the tax authorities to make their full pension scheme applicable under the age of 55 but they are confident that it will come down to 50 within the next ten years – well in time for the generation now starting their careers.

There will always be the glorious exceptions of course, while those who control their own careers, the self-employed, the professions and, apparently, Heads of State, will buck the trend as long as the clients and their supporters will permit it. It is the bigger organizations, in which most full-timers still work, who will be most choosy about who they keep on their full-time books and they will want the energetic, the up-to-date, the committed and the flexible. Most of those will be in their thirties and forties, putting in their 50,000 hours in big annual chunks.

Full-time work in organizations will, however, be only one of the options and, if the numbers are anything like right, it will be a minority option, perhaps an élite one. Most people will have to find their place outside the organization, selling their time or their services into it, as self-employed, part-time or temporary workers.

For them the pattern of hours will be different. They may find themselves working 25 hours a week for 45 weeks of the year (part-time) or 45 hours a week for 25 weeks a year (temporary). In either case they will need to keep on working so long as they can, for 45 years if possible, because they will not be able to accumulate the savings via pension schemes or other mechanisms to live on. This will suit the organizations who will, in their temporary staff, look for experience and reliability rather than the energy and certainty of youth. Whether it is temporary work or part-time work, the sum is still $25 \times 45 \times 45 = 50,000$.

We may, therefore, see the notional retirement age going in two very different ways at the same time. Whilst for the core workers it will gradually come down towards 50 over the next twenty years, for most of the workforce it will go up. For them the questions 'What shall I do in the missing 50,000 hours, and what shall I live on?' cannot be postponed until the Third Age; they need to be answered now. For these people the future is not a generation away – it started yesterday.

My children have a fourth option. They may be able to work full-time for ten years, then take ten years out to raise a family, then return to the workforce at, say, 45 for a further ten or even fifteen years. ($45 \times 45 \times 25$ hours of paid work = 50,000.) It is an option that has traditionally been taken up by women, who have varied the pattern by going part-time for some of the intervening years, but it may increasingly be seen as an opportunity by men to vary their lifestyle and to play a bigger part in the home and family life.

Re-entry into the full-time workforce has always been difficult. It will get easier as the shortage of qualified young people begins to bite organizations in the 1990s. The organization will then turn to that reservoir of talent, the qualified women at home. In order to tempt them back, however, organizations may have to learn to be more flexible in the way they run things, more willing to recognize that they are buying the talents of someone but not necessarily all their time.

The Pressures Behind The Numbers

The $\frac{100,000}{2} (4) = J$ equation is, of course, spuriously precise.

The numbers will not work out precisely like that. It is there to make a point. The world of jobs is changing. It is changing more dramatically than we realize because those sort of numbers creep up on one unexpectedly when multiplied out over a lifetime.

No one particularly wants those numbers to happen. They are not the result of any policy decisions by government or boards of directors. They are an instinctive response to a changing environment. There is now some general agreement about the nature of this changing environment and an acceptance that it is not going to change back again. Some of the main features are:

A move away from labour-intensive manufacturing
Thirty years ago nearly half of all workers in the industrialized countries were making or helping to make *things*. In another thirty years' time it may be down to 10 per cent (in the USA it is already 18 per cent).

To some extent this is because we have all had to export our factories, instead of our goods, to countries where labour is cheaper and more amenable to factory working. Even Japan has now been forced by the high price of the yen to follow suit. When Britain did not export her factories soon enough they were replicated in the newly industrialized countries and she lost out. Situations such as the rapid rise of the pound sterling in the early years of Margaret Thatcher's government only accelerated this process, leaving swathes of abandoned factories throughout Britain. It would have happened anyway. The clever thing would have been not to compete with the unbeatable but to join them by exporting the factories not the goods. Discontinuous change can always be turned to advantage with a bit of forethought.

The result is not just fewer jobs, but different organizations. Labour-intensive manufacturing was traditionally managed with a large pool of relatively cheap labour, a lot of supervision and a hierarchical management structure. There were a lot of people around, most of them full-time employees whose time was bought to be used at the discretion of the organization, subject increasingly to the agreement of the union.

It was a convenient way to run things; everything and everyone you needed was yours. If you want to control it, own it, was the message. It proved, in the end, to be a very expensive message. The Japanese always did it differently, with a small core staff, a raft of subcontractors, heavy investment in clever machines and enough clever people to instruct them and work with them. The demise of mass manufacturing has led to the end of the mass employment organization and with it a redefinition of the job.

A move towards knowledge-based organizations
The end of labour-intensive manufacturing leaves us with organizations which receive their added value from the

knowledge and the creativity they put in rather than the muscle-power. Fewer people, thinking better, helped by clever machines and computers, add more value than gangs or lines of unthinking 'human resources'. Manufacturing has gone this way. The more obviously knowledge-based businesses of consultancy, finance and insurance, advertising, journalism and publishing, television, health care, education and entertainment, have all flourished. Even agriculture and construction, the oldest of industries, have invested in knowledge and clever machines in place of muscles.

The result is not only a requirement for different people, but different organizations, organizations which recognize that they cannot do everything themselves, that they need a central group of talented and energetic people, a lot of specialist help and ancillary agencies. They are smaller, younger organizations than their predecessors, flatter and less hierarchical. We shall examine them in more detail in the following chapters, but their most immediate effect is on the numbers – fewer people inside who are better qualified, more people outside who are contracted not employed.

A move towards service

Paradoxically, rich societies seem to breed dependency. If you are poor you are forced into self-sufficiency. As you get rich it is easier and more sensible to get other people to do what you do not want to do or cannot do, be it fixing the roof or digging the garden. It makes economic sense to let others make your clothes and to buy them in the store, that way you get better clothes and more time to do what you are good at. It goes on and on. Convenience foods take the chore out of cooking, and package holidays the work out of leisure. We all of us become more specialized, better at one thing and worse at others. Like knowledge-based organizations we contract out everything we are not good at and so breed a raft of services on which we now depend.

Affluence breeds service industries and they in turn create affluence. Sometimes it seems as if everyone is taking in everyone else's metaphorical washing and making money out of it, or in my particular case, that everyone is going to everyone else's conference and being paid for it or paying for it. Affluence is a matter of mood and self-confidence as much as of economics, for dependency has its own imperatives. If you need to buy all these services you have to find something to do to pay for them, hence some competitive striving. It is a self-fulfilling prophecy which works as long as everyone believes the prophecy of continued affluence.

The service industries of affluence are therefore ephemeral creations, which could always disappear overnight. The point however, once again, is that the organizations which they spawn are of a different kind. Because they are essentially ephemeral they have to flex with every shift in demand. Small core staff and lots of part-time and temporary help has to be the rule. Many of them are not knowledge-intensive businesses, although some are, of course. Retailing, transport, cleaning, catering, leisure, are all industries with large requirements for the competent but semi-skilled. It is here that you will find most of the 30 per cent who do not have the brain skills for the knowledge-based organizations. It is here that you will find the bulk of the part-timers and the temporary workers.

It is the growth of the service sector which has transformed the working lives of so many people in Europe and the USA *because* of the kind of organization which it needs and breeds.

These shifts are irreversible. The degree of affluence may increase or wane in each country but labour-intensive manufacturing will not return to Europe, or to the USA and Japan. Knowledge-based enterprises have to be the way forward for all our countries, the more and the better the richer, whether they are manufacturing goods or providing services. The service sector will ebb and flow with local prosperity but will never now fade away.

If the shifts are irreversible so are the changes in the patterns of work which they induce, and therefore the numbers with which this chapter began. A dramatic change in the economic climate may slow things down, but it will not stop them. The world of work has changed already. We need to take notice.

3   The Theory

The message, I hope, is clear: the times are changing and we must change with them. Yes, but how? In Chapter 1 I argued that because most people do not like change, change is forced upon them by crisis and discontinuity. Thrown up against things, or into new arenas, we confront new possibilities and discover bits of ourselves we never knew were there. Discontinuity is a great learning experience, but only if we survive it.

My daughter was smitten by an unexplained viral illness earlier this year. She is 22. These illnesses knock the stuffing out of the sufferer and she had to drop everything for a year – work, friends, study, even the television. It was, for her, a massive discontinuity and profoundly depressing. Getting better slowly she went to a meeting one evening on 'Gratitude'. 'If they had asked me to speak,' she told me, 'I would have said that I was grateful for my illness. I have learnt so much.' And changed so much, I wanted to add.

Change, however, does not have to be forced on us by crisis and calamity. We can do it for ourselves. If changing is, as I have argued, only another word for learning, then the theories of learning will also be theories of changing. Those who are always learning are those who can ride the waves of change and who see a changing world as full of opportunities not damages. They are the ones most likely to be the survivors in a time of discontinuity. They are also the enthusiasts and the architects of new ways and forms and ideas. If you want to change, try learning one might say, or more precisely, if you want to be in control of your change, take learning more seriously. This chapter, therefore, is an introduction to the theory of learning, which is the theory at the heart of changing.

'A theory of learning?' the Professor of Medicine said to me when he heard what I was writing, 'I never knew there was such a thing.' It is indeed ironic that those who teach us, particularly in our universities, are so often ignorant of the basic principles of learning. The Professor had never heard of Kolb, who first convinced me that learning is a cycle of different activities, although I have used different words from his in this chapter. Nor had he heard of Bateson or of Argyris and Schon who persuaded me that learning is a double loop, that there is learning to solve a particular problem and then, more importantly, there is the habit of learning, the learning to learn to do such things, that second loop which can change the way you live. He knew not of Revans, the unsung hero of Action Learning, who showed me that the best learning happens in real life with real problems and real people and not in classrooms with know-all teachers. There were others, too, he knew not, Dewey who said, many years ago, that learning was a process of discovery and that we must each be our own discoverer, others could not do it for you; or Illich who thought that we would be better off without schools which were concerned with indoctrination not teaching. He had, sadly, heard a bit about Skinner who believes that learning is training, that teaching is producing a conditioned response as when your dog responds to your whistle.

There are many others, for learning has intrigued mankind for centuries. This chapter is my personal anthology, turned into my own images and metaphors, for reasons which will, I hope, become clear.

A Theory Of Learning

The man stood in front of the class. 'Now learn this,' he said, writing an equation on the board. We wrote it in our books. Three months later we wrote it out again in an examination paper. If the second time of writing was the same as the first, we had learnt it. I exaggerate, but only a little. That was my early concept of learning. Later on, I came to realize that I had learnt nothing at school which I now remember except only this – that all problems had already been solved, by someone, and that the answer was around, in the back of the book or the teacher's head. Learning seemed to mean transferring answers from them to me.

There was nothing about change in all of that. Nor, in fact, was there much about learning as it really is. Real learning, I came to understand, is always about answering a question or solving a problem. 'Who am I?' 'How do I do this?' 'What is the reason for ...?' 'How does this work?' 'How do I achieve this ambition?' The questions range from the immense to the trivial, but when we have no questions we need no answers, while other people's questions are soon forgotten.

It is best, I realized, to think of learning as a wheel divided into four parts:

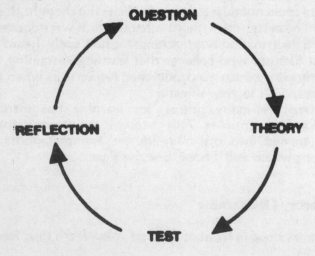

I draw it as a wheel to emphasize that it is meant to go round and round. One set of questions, duly answered and tested and reflected upon, leads on to another. It is life's special treadmill. Step off it and you ossify, and become a bore to others. The trouble is that for most of us for much of the time the wheel does *not* go round. It gets stuck or blocked.

Mankind, I am sure, is born to learn. One has only to look at little children to see that wheel turning furiously. Why, we must wonder, does it slow down for most of us as we grow older? If we knew more about that we would know more about our reluctance to change and the consequent need for crisis and calamity to budge us into action. This chapter, therefore, is really about the things in us and in our surroundings which *stop* or *block* the wheel. First, however, we need a brief introduction to the wheel itself.

The Wheel of Learning
Logically, the wheel starts with a *question*, a problem to be solved, a dilemma to be resolved, a challenge to meet. If it doesn't start there, and if it is not *our* question, we shall not push the wheel round to the stage of Reflection. It won't become part of us. I could learn a poem by heart at school to recite the next morning, but to forget by lunchtime. This was learning to answer *other* people's questions. Just occasionally the poem would touch some chord in me, some unspoken question; it would provide some clue to the emerging mystery of life – those poems I remember still. The question, in other words, does not have to be some kind of examination question, more often it is a sort of reaching for, a questioning, a need to explore. Learning is discovery, Dewey said, but discovery doesn't happen unless you are looking. Necessity may be the mother of invention but curiosity is the mother of discovery.

Questions need possible answers. The next stage provides them. *Theories* is too grand a term. I use it only to emphasize that this stage is investigating *possible* ideas. It is a stage of speculation, of free-thinking, of re-framing, of looking for clues. One way is to open the equivalent of a cookbook or, in my case, a series of cookbooks in search of that elusive formula which will produce a culinary miracle in half-an-hour from my random collection of left-overs. There are other ways to find possible answers; good friends, hired coaches, or even one's own imagination.

Ideas and Theories can never be enough. At this stage of the wheel all is still fancy. 'Dreams,' as my children used to remind me, 'give wings to fools.' The theories have to be *tested* in reality, the next stage of the wheel. Some will work, some won't. My sauce is always lumpy – why? Until I know why, which is the stage of *Reflection*, the final stage, I will not have learnt. Change only sticks when we understand why it happened. Too often have I invited chief executives to explain their philosophy only to listen to a bare record of their achievements, with no interpretation, no theory to explain them, no philosophy expounded. Such men have not changed and will not change. They have learnt nothing from their success which makes it unlikely that they will be able to repeat it.

The wheel, however, is difficult to turn. For some it never gets started. They have no questions and seek no answers. Content or dull depending on your viewpoint, they will not voluntarily learn or change.

There are those, too, who stick at the Question stage. Like small children they delight in asking why, or how, or when, or where, and as long as they get an answer, any answer, they are satisfied for it is the questions which fascinate them, not the answer. They don't learn and others don't learn much from their questions. They are life's Inspectors or Auditors; useful, no doubt, but irritating.

The next stage, Theory, has its own specialists. They are the bad Academics, full of answers to other people's questions. They teach the answer first and assume the question. Knowledge for its own sake is what motivates these people, they are fact-collectors who know a lot and have, in a fuller sense, learnt little. I have a friend who turns every conversation into a lecture, on anything. He has read a lot and forgotten nothing and is eager to share it with anyone who will listen. At last I have learnt how to enjoy his company, to come with a question to which *I* wanted an answer and which he could always provide.

The Testing stage has its own enthusiasts, the Action Men or Pragmatists. No time for theory or for thinking, their immediate reaction to a problem is to attack it with the tools nearest to hand. Energy conquers all, they believe, and if at first it doesn't work, try and try again. Often it does work. The trouble is they don't know why. 'I kick it, that usually does the trick' is their formula. Success without prior thought or subsequent reflection does not help you to repeat the process or to improve on it, although it does get the problem moving. They can be effective, these pragmatists, but find it hard to communicate their secret to other people because they have not gone through the other segments of the wheel.

Lastly there are those who get stuck at the Reflection stage. Endlessly they rehearse the past, seeking for better explanations of what went wrong or what went right. They are the Pundits amongst us. They have learnt because they have been round the wheel but there they have stopped. One lesson is enough; they have made up their minds and feel no need for further explanation. Busy people often have no time for more curiosity. They formed their opinions long ago and see no cause to change them. 'Consistent' we call them if we agree with them, 'bigots' if we don't.

Most of the time, most of us do not go through all the four segments of this wheel. I describe it here to emphasize how difficult true learning is and why the sort of deliberate change that goes with learning is so rare. This sort of learning, the one from experience and life, is the one that matters if we are to change. It is not to be confused with more trivial definitions of learning:

— Learning is *not* just knowing the answers. That is *Mastermind* learning at its best, rote learning at its most boring and conditioned response at its most basic. It does not help you to change or to grow, it does not move the wheel.
— Learning is *not* the same as study, nor the same as training. It is bigger than both. It is a cast of mind, a habit of life, a way of thinking about things, a way of growing.
— Learning is *not* measured by examinations, which usually only test the Theory stage, but only by a growing experience, an experience understood and tested.
— Learning is *not* automatic, it requires energy, thought, courage and support. It is easy to give up on it, to relax and to rest on one's experience, but that is to cease to grow.
— Learning is *not* only for the intellectuals, who often shine at the thinking stage, but are incurious and unadventurous and therefore add little to their experience as they go through life.
— Learning is *not* finding out what other people already know, but is solving our own problems for our own purposes, by questioning, thinking and testing until the solution is a new part of our life.

The Lubricants Of Change

The wheel of learning, I have emphasized, is difficult to start and hard to keep moving. Most of us don't succeed most of the time. We get stuck at one or other segment and only a crisis or calamity can then move us on. Luckily there are some lubricants which make it easier - 'the necessary conditions of comfortable change'. There are three of these lubricants, each of which needs some interpretation. Leave them out or screen them out and change or learning is effectively blocked.

1. A proper selfishness

This is a responsible selfishness. I am often tempted to observe that the Christian injunction to love one's neighbour as oneself gives the neighbour a rather poor deal since few people seem to love or even like themselves that much.

Unfortunately, however, self-hate or just a lack of some 'positive self-regard' is no way to start learning. I am not advocating a narcissistic self-indulgence. I am suggesting, on the basis of good evidence, that those who learn best and most, and change most comfortably, are those who

(a) take responsibility for themselves and for their future;
(b) have a clear view of what they want that future to be;
(c) want to make sure that they get it; and
(d) believe that they can.

It looks easy. It seldom is. Taking a view of one's future requires, first of all, that you believe that there will be a future. There are times, for all of us, when that seems doubtful. In those moods there is no learning, no changing. Then there is the question of what sort of future would we like it to be, for us. Sensibly, selfishly, it should fit our talents and our abilities, but we are sometimes the last people to know what those are. It should not be a fantasy future – that is escapism, but what *is* reality, we may well ask.

The exercises at the end of this chapter are intended as one way to focus attention on these intractable questions. We may never get the answers right but unless we take a view we shall be mere flotsam on the waves of life. Fred Hirsch, an economist and philosopher, described what happens to many people under a pervasive materialism. We end up, he suggested, not by working for what we *need* but for what we *want*, for the 'positional goods' that keep us abreast or ahead of the notional Joneses. It's a no-win situation for there will always be more Joneses to keep up with. It is unthinking, follow-my-neighbour, selfishness, not proper self-responsibility.

2. *A way of re-framing*
The second of the lubricants or necessary conditions is particularly useful in the second stage of the wheel of learning. Re-framing is the ability to see things, problems, situations or people in other ways, to look at them sideways, or upside-down; to put them in another perspective or another context; to think of them as opportunities not problems, as hiccups rather than disasters.

Re-framing is important because it unlocks problems. Like an unexpected move on a chessboard it can give the whole situation a new look. It is akin to lateral thinking at times, to using the right side of the brain (the creative pattern-forming side) to complement the more logical left side.

To conceive of one's life without the word 'retirement' being relevant is to re-frame it. To think of a job as 2000 hours in a year instead of 45 weeks of 5 long days is to re-frame it, and by so doing to open up new possibilities. A federal organization is a re-framing of a decentralized organization, with important consequences.

In business it has long been fashionable to ask 'What business are you in?' Is it cigarettes you are selling, or stress reducers, or social ease, or just a drug? The re-framing will have important consequences for the way the product is projected, distributed and priced.

Entrepreneurs, when they are successful, often achieve their success through intuitive re-framing, connecting what was before unconnected, putting together an opportunity and a need.

I remember the year when Britain was short of potatoes – the last year there was a drought. A friend and I went shopping for potatoes only to find there were none. Weeks later he asked me what I had done as a result.

'Bought rice instead,' I said. 'Why?'

'I rang a contact in India,' he replied, 'bought one thousand tons of potatoes to be shipped to the UK at a landed cost of £130 a ton and sold them in advance for £250 a ton.'

'But, Percy,' I said, calculating quickly, 'that's ...'

'Yes,' he interrupted, 'but don't worry, it didn't happen, the Indians refused an export permit.'

Still, his re-framing nearly made him £120,000, while I bought rice.

Businesses, at their best, re-frame all the time, re-thinking what they now call their portfolios of mini-businesses, re-defining those businesses, and their markets, checking to make sure that there are as many growing businesses as declining ones. Individuals need to do the same, looking at their portfolios of talents, recognizing that what might be a disadvantage in one situation could be an asset in another, as when Mary realized that her problem – she could only talk naturally to people when she didn't have to look at them – made her a natural for telephone selling.

Some people are natural re-framers. Most of us cannot do it alone. Other people always help. Friendly groups help one to re-think the problem or the situation. It helps if they are people outside the problem because they will bring different ideas to bear. Group-think is dangerous because like-minded groups have like-minded ideas and find it hard amongst themselves to re-frame any situation.

I am a great believer in 'Irish Education' after the Irishman who reputedly said, 'How do I know what I think until I hear what I say?' Truth, said David Hume, the Scottish philo-sopher, springs from argument amongst friends. Even if we don't convince the friends, we often help ourselves to see things in a new way as we look for new angles in the argument.

Metaphors and analogies help. Schon's idea of the 'displacement of concepts' mentioned in Chapter 1 as an aid to creativity is a useful discipline, to try to find other metaphors, or words from other fields, to describe the problem or the dilemma. There are other drills and disciplines to stretch the mind, most usefully in some of Edward de Bono's books.

We are all the prisoners of our past. It is hard to think of things except in the way we have always thought of them. But that way solves no problems and seldom changes anything. It is certainly no way to deal with discontinuity. We must accustom ourselves to asking 'Why?' of what already is and 'Why not?' to any possible re-framing. It can become a useful game.

For instance, why do women take their husband's name when they marry? Why not keep their own, or both choose a new common name? Why do we make marriage vows for ever, and then break them? Why not make them for shorter terms, and then renew them? Why do so many houses have their best rooms in the front, looking over the parking space? Why not put all entrances at the side? And so on . . .

Upside-down thinking, re-framing, is largely a habit of mind. Those who want to learn in life, and to change comfortably, need to practise it.

3. A Negative Capability

Keats defined 'negative capability' in his letters in 1817, as 'when a man is capable of being in uncertainties, mysteries, and doubts'. I would extend the meaning to include the capacity to live with mistakes and failures without being downhearted or dismayed.

Learning and changing are never clear and never sure. Whenever we change we step out a little into the unknown.

We will never know enough about that unknown to be certain of the result. We will get it wrong some of the time. Doubt and mistakes must not be allowed to disturb us because it is from them that we learn. Theories are no good, Karl Popper argued, unless it is possible to prove them wrong. If they are bound to be right they are either tautologies, saying nothing useful, or trivial, saying nothing important.

Entrepreneurs, the successful ones, have on average nine failures for every success. It is only the successes that you will hear about, the failures they credit to experience. Oil companies expect to drill nine empty wells for every one that flows. Getting it wrong is part of getting it right. As with my friend and the potatoes, if you do not try you will not succeed and if it fails, there is always another day, another opportunity. Negative capability is an attitude of mind which learners need to cultivate, to help them to write off their mistakes as experience. It helps to get your first failures early on; the later ones are then less painful. Those who have a gilded youth, in which success leads on to success, are sometimes the least experimental and the most conservative as they grow older because the fear of failure looms larger.

We were about to appoint a new Professor. The person in question was well-known to us, a brilliant lecturer, an authority in his field, a sought-after consultant. Why then were there so many unspoken reservations in the faces around the table? Someone then captured it for us: 'The trouble is,' he said, 'Richard has no decent doubt.' Without that decent doubt there was no questioning, no learning, no deliberate change. To Richard, certainty was precious, a negative capability something he would not understand.

We learn by our mistakes, as we always tell ourselves, not from our successes; but perhaps we do not really believe it. We should, for we change by exploration not by retracing well-known paths. We start our learning with uncertainties and doubts, with questions to be resolved. We grow older wondering who we will be and what we will do. For organizations as for individuals life is a book still to be written. If we cannot live with these uncertainties we will not learn and change will always be an unpleasant surprise.

Negative capability, that capacity to live with uncertainty and mistake, is not given to everyone. Keats complained that Coleridge did not have it and missed a trick or two thereby. It helps, clearly, to have a belief that overrides the uncertainty. For some it is a feeling that their book of life is already written, that they are merely turning the pages. For others it is a belief in a superior being, a God. For myself, I have become convinced of the truth behind the Coda of Julian of Norwich, a holy lady in fourteenth century Britain: 'All will be well, and all manner of thing will be well', she said, again and again. Believe that, although one cannot know in what way all will be well, and a negative capability is easy.

The Blocks To Change

It is, unfortunately, all too easy to stop the lubricants reaching the wheel. A proper selfishness, re-framing and a negative capability are fragile. It is easier to stop them than to encourage them, often unintentionally. The principal blocks are listed here.

The 'They' syndrome
Mary was divorcing her army husband. Where would she live, I asked, when she had to leave her army apartment. 'They haven't told me yet,' she said.

'Who are they?' I asked.

'They haven't told me who they are yet, have they?' she replied, irritated at my seeming stupidity.

It is easy to laugh but once I waited outside the door of the Personnel Manager of the multinational company of my youth. A wily old Scot passed by, a veteran of that place and a wise counsellor.

'What are you waiting for, laddie?' he asked.

'I am waiting to see what they are planning for me.'

'Och, invest in yourself, my boy, don't wait for them. Invest in yourself, if you don't why should they?'

It was one of those timely triggers. Until that moment I was leaving it all to 'them', I had no sense of personal responsibility for my own future. That had been delegated to the Personnel Department. 'They' would tell me. Unfortunately, 'they' wondered why I had been so lackadaisical about my own development and did not, as Jock forecast, see any great reason to continue their investment in my future unless I also invested in it.

Too many delegate their futures and their questions to some mysterious 'they'. 'They' will set the syllabus for life just as 'they' set the syllabus for our courses at school. 'They' know what is best, 'they' must know what they are doing. 'They' are in charge, leave it to 'them'. The phrases and excuses are endless. One of the strange things about growing older is the gradual realization that 'they' don't know, that the Treasury is *not* all-wise, that 'they' are on the whole just like you, muddling through, and not very interested in you anyway.

Futility/humility

Learning starts with a belief in oneself. It is for all of us a fragile belief, easily shattered. In my early days in that big company, I found myself in Malaysia with, effectively, a license to wander through the departments. I came across what seemed to me to be some gross inefficiencies. I worked out some better options, sent them to the Operations Manager and waited – for his thanks. He sent for me.

'How long have you been out here?' he asked.

'Six months,' I replied.

'And how long has this company been successfully doing business here?'

'About fifty years, I suppose.'

'Quite so, fifty-four in fact; and do you suppose that in six months you know better than the rest of us and our predecessors in fifty-four years?'

I asked no more questions for the next three years, had no more ideas, made no more proposals. My social life prospered, I recall, but I stopped learning, and growing, and changing.

If one remark killed my belief in myself in that place, one can easily work out why it is that the unemployed or the newly redundant have little urge or energy to turn that wheel of learning. All *they* want is to turn the clock back and to have the same job again. We have made the 'job' so essential to a man's concept of himself, and now to many a woman's, that the loss of it, often through no fault of his own, can shatter his sense of identity, of personal worth, of self-esteem, for a while at least.

Self-doubt is pernicious. Humble, self-doubting people, may ask the questions but they do not press for answers or for action. 'Others need or deserve it more than I' they say, seeking always the back of the queue even if the queue is really only a huddle. John needs my help, the firm cannot spare me, my needs can wait. The selfishness is laudable, often, but the learning gets postponed. Other people become a prop for or an excuse for our lack of self-responsibility.

Self-doubters often fear success. Success puts more pressure on them to take more responsibility for even more action. Failure for some is easier to handle, particularly if you plan for it. David, his teachers noted, although a clever boy, had stopped working some months before his big exams. They tried to coax him back to work with forecasts of what he might achieve. They tried to frighten him with forecasts of what he might *not* achieve. Nothing worked. He did as badly as they feared, but he had his excuse, he had done no work. His failure was not an indictment of his ability but only of his attitude. His own conception of himself as a clever lad, was untouched. They call it a form of 'attribution theory'; it is a way of dodging failure, of not learning in order to protect a fragile sense of self. He won't start to learn again until he is strong enough in his self-confidence to take success *or* failure in his stride.

The theft of purposes

Proper, responsible selfishness, involves a purpose and a goal. It is that goal which pulls out the energy to move the wheel. Diminish that goal, displace it or, worst of all, disallow it and we remove all incentive to learn or to change. Proper selfishness, however, recognizes that the goal needs to be tuned to the goals of the group, or the organization, or society, as well as being in line with our own needs and our own talents. Only improper selfishness sets goals at odds with the bits of humanity that matter to oneself.

It is tempting to impose our goals on other people, particularly on children or our subordinates. It is tempting for society to try to impose its priorities on everybody. The strategy will however be self-defeating if our goals, or society's goals, do not fit the goals of the others. We may get our way but we don't get their learning. They may have to comply but they will not change. We have pushed out their goals with ours and stolen their purposes. It is a pernicious form of theft which kills the will to learn. The apathy and disillusion of many people in organizations, the indifference and apparent indolence of the unemployed is often due to the fact that there is no room for their purposes or goals in our scheme of things. Left goal-less, they comply, drift or rebel.

In a sensible world the goals are negotiated. The concept of the do'nut in Chapter 5 allows the organization to dictate the core and the perimeter of one's role, but allows discretion in the middle with the purposes of that discretion to be agreed. It is so, or could be so, with much of life. Responsible selfishness knows that there are core duties and necessary boundaries but also that there must be room for self-expression. Squeeze it out, as tidy-minded bureaucrats so often do, and we kill any motivation to learn.

The missing forgiveness

I asked an American the secret of his firm's obviously successful development policy. He looked me straight in the eye. 'Forgiveness,' he said. 'We give them big jobs and big responsibilities. Inevitably they make mistakes, we can't check them all the time and don't want to. They learn, we forgive, they don't make the mistake again.'

He was unusual. Too many organizations use their appraisal schemes and their confidential files to record our errors and our small disasters. They use them to chastise us with, hoping to inspire us, or to frighten us to do better. It might work once but in future we will make sure that we do not venture far enough from the beaten track to make any mistake. Yet no experiment, no test of new ideas, means no learning and no change. As in organizations, so it can be in families.

The evidence is quite consistent, if you reward the good and ignore or forgive the bad, the good will occur more frequently and the bad will gradually disappear. A concern over trouble in the classroom led to research into the way teachers allocated praise and blame. About equally, it seemed, except that all praise was for academic work and all blame was for behaviour. The teachers were coached to *only* give praise, for both academic work and good behaviour and to *ignore* the bad. It worked. Within a few weeks unruly behaviour had almost disappeared.

More difficult than forgiving others is to forgive oneself. That turns out to be one of the real blocks to change. We as individuals need to accept our past but then to turn our backs on it. Organizations often do it by changing their name, individuals by moving house, or changing spouses. It does not have to be so dramatic. Scrapbooks, I believe, are useful therapy – they are a way of putting the past to bed, decorously. Then we can move forward.

Putting The Theory To Work

If we want to change comfortably and deliberately we each have to start turning our own personal wheel of learning. The lubricants will make it easier – some proper selfishness, a constant effort to re-frame our bit of the world, and a readiness to forgive yourself.

Give yourself space, a purpose and goals to reach, questions to answer: find some friends to be your mentors, walk in other worlds, don't be afraid to be wrong.

It is, of course, easier to write or say than to do. Some exercises help, if you can organize yourself to do them and to use a partner or a friend to help you reflect upon them.

Exercise 1

Draw a line on a piece of paper to represent your life, from birth to death, and mark with a cross where you are now on that line. Think about it a bit, but not for too long; this is an impressionistic exercise not a precise one. Most people will draw a line something like the one below. Do yours before you read on.

In effect it is a line over time going up and down. What, however, do the ups and downs represent? The answer will tell you something about your real priorities in life. Where did you put the cross? The position will tell you something about the proportion of your life which you still feel is ahead of you, with time, probably, for a good Third Age. Does the line go upwards at the end or downwards? The answer will tell you something about your secret thoughts about the future. Most people feel good about it, in some modified way, and point their lines upwards.

Exercise 2

Write your own obituary to appear in your favourite paper or journal. Assume that it is written by a good friend who knows you well and understands the 'you' behind the facts. Don't write more than 200 words.

People find this difficult to do but useful if they do it and then show it to a good friend. It is difficult because it requires you to envisage your own death as a real event. To be able to do this can be a big release because it allows you to think in more concrete terms about the long period between now and your death.

The exercise forces you to stand at the end of your life and to look backwards. It puts what you are doing now into a new perspective and forces you to work out what you would like to be remembered for. It is an exercise in very personal re-framing.

Exercise 3

Imagine yourself asking ten friends to list one quality each which they liked or admired in you. List those qualities, then against each list two activities where those qualities *have* been useful in the past and one type of different activity where they *could* conceivably be useful. Better still, ask ten friends to do it for you.

It is difficult to do this objectively by yourself, but worth trying. The point is to accentuate the positive in you and to conceive of other areas where your talents might be useful. It is, in a small way, a practice in liking yourself.

Exercise 4

Now, and only now, having done the others, list five things you would like to have achieved in three years' time. Describe in a little detail how the achievement will be measured or observable and set down what practical things need to be done to start work on them.

This, of course, is putting the wheel of learning and of deliberate change into motion. It is surprising how easy it can be to do what we want to do when we know what it is that we want. Changing is exciting, fun and not too difficult if we see it as learning, learning in my sense, learning that we control and that we want.

I am more and more sure that those who are in love with learning are in love with life. For them change is never a problem, never a threat, just another exciting opportunity. It does, however, require what you might call a positive mental attitude.

Earlier this year we had to move out of our home for nine months while urgent repairs were made to the foundations. It was going to be a great nuisance and inconvenience. At first we were minded to minimize the inconvenience and camp out in makeshift accommodation next door. Then we decided to turn it into an opportunity, an opportunity to live in another part of town in a very different sort of home and community, to treat it like a foreign posting. It was more inconvenient, but now we call it exciting, fun, adventure and a bit of positive learning. Bad news became good news, change was learning.

Part Two: Working

Introduction

'He is 55 and he has just experienced his first month for 37 years without a paycheque. He is depressed, impossible to live with and I'm at my wits end.' It was a middle-class wife speaking. They were not poor because with early retirement had come an early pension, they owned their home and their children were independent. It was not even that he had enjoyed his job. He had, in fact, despised it but, masochistically, had borne his dislike of his work like a man. Remove it and, paradoxically, he began to doubt his manhood.

Later that day I ring another friend, also 55. His voice on an answerphone replies 'Anderson Associates – Paul Anderson speaking, I am contactable on 036484911.' I know that the Associates are he and his wife and occasional friends in his or her multifarious little enterprises, some of which make money, many of which don't. I know that the other telephone number is a fishing lodge belonging to some friends where he likes to spend long summer days. I know that his wife, a freelance journalist since the children grew up, makes more money than him, that their kitchen is their office. I know that for her and him, now, work and fun are inextricably intertwined, that he would never go back to working in a bank, that the telephone and the new opportunities for little service enterprises have transformed both their lives.

That evening my children, now in their early twenties, bring round some friends. The jobs they are doing did not exist in my youth – a production assistant in a small video company, a courier, a pop musician, a bond dealer in the city.

There was also the perpetual traveller and the endless student, living rather precariously off odd-jobs, a grant and the occasional cheque from the welfare office. They none of them expected their job or their lifestyle to stay that way for long. The twenties were a time of exploration, for discovering the world and themselves. Careers were middle-aged concepts, things of the 1970s. Money mattered to them, but money was earnable if you wanted it enough and if you put your mind to it, and there were other parts of life which did not depend on money. They were both more carefree and more caring for others than I was at their age; they were less bound to their jobs than I was but often put more energy into the actual work. It was loyalty to the work, not to the employer which mattered most.

But then there was the young man I had heard being interviewed on the radio that morning. He had left school at 16 and was now 23. No educational credits, no qualifications, no sense of personal talents. He had never had a job but felt let down, cheated, by a society that had seemed to promise him the right to work and to a wage. By now he was without ambition, had a child by a girl whom he had not married, was drifting with no plan for the future. When asked if he had thought of enrolling on one of the many training courses or schemes which are now available, he replied that he was no good at that sort of thing and that anyway they were only a politician's scheme for cutting down the number of unemployed.

The stories are familiar. They are happening all over Europe and in the USA. Some are those of happiness and good fortune. Some are of depression and even of hopelessness. They are the stories of discontinuous change at work, of those that adapt, even rejoice in the opportunity, and of those who lose their way and their will. Sometimes it seems that whole slices of generations have been allotted to pay the price for the mammoth change in the places of work which has taken place over the past twenty years and will continue for at least another ten. The Numbers (Chapter 2) have made clear how mammoth is that change; the next three chapters in Part Two describe and explain what it looks like.

4 The Shamrock Organization

The world of work is changing because the organizations of work are changing their ways. At the same time, however, the organizations are having to adapt to a changing world of work. It's a chicken and egg situation. One thing, at least, is clear – organizations in both private and public sectors face a tougher world – one in which they are judged more harshly than before on their effectiveness and in which there are fewer protective hedges behind which to shelter. It applies to hospitals and schools and employment offices as much as it does to businesses of all sorts.

It has been made increasingly clear, in Britain at least, that it is the organization's job to deliver; it is not its job to be everyone's alternative community, providing meaning and work for all for life; nor is its job to be another arm of the state, collecting its taxes, paying the pensions, employing the handicapped and the disadvantaged, administering an implicit incomes policy or collaborating with an exchange rate policy. They have been very convenient, these employment organizations, as the delivery instruments of government policy but now that they employ, full-time, an ever-decreasing percentage of society's adults they have become less useful. The alternative community idea has also got in the way, some people believe, of the organizations' proper job which is to deliver quality goods and services to their customers. 'My social objectives add five per cent to my costs,' one chief executive said to me recently, complainingly.

It all begs a huge question, of course. If the organizations are no longer expected to look after people, then who is? It is a question which was raised in the first chapter of this book; it will come up again. My concern in this part, however, is to examine how organizations have begun to respond to this increased pressure for results, and how their ways and their requirements of their people are now hugely different - discontinuous change has begun to happen, for good as well as for ill.

It is not just that results matter more and that there is more scope for radical change in the way they are delivered; the organizations of today are more and more places for brains not muscles. As we saw, brain skills will be required in 70 per cent of all jobs, according to one very believable forecast, and perhaps half of those brain skill jobs will require professional qualifications or education up to university degree level. These are increasingly organizations of clever people doing clever things, and clever people have to be managed rather more sensitively than in the days when factories were manned by 'hands'.

One sign of the new sorts of organization is a perceptible change in the language we use to talk about them. Organizations used to be perceived as gigantic pieces of engineering, with largely interchangeable human parts. We talked of their structures and their systems, of inputs and outputs, of control devices and of managing them, as if the whole was one large factory. Today the language is not that of engineering but of politics, with talk of cultures and networks, of teams and coalitions, of influence or power rather than control, of leadership not management. It is as if we had suddenly woken up to the fact that organizations were made up of people, after all, not just 'hands' or 'role occupants'. It is, thinking about it, a startling discontinuity even if it has crept up on most of us unnoticed.

The new thinking on organizations shows itself in several ways, in the shamrock organization, the new alliance of different types of work and worker (discussed in this chapter), in the federal organization, the new form of the organization with its interesting counterpart, the do'nut concept of management (discussed in Chapter 5), in the smart organization and the shake-up that is happening as a consequence to the careers and lives of managers (discussed in Chapter 6). Discontinuities at work do, in the end, affect what we do on Monday morning.

The Idea Of The Shamrock

The shamrock is the Irish national emblem, a small clover-like plant with three leaves to each stem. It was used by St Patrick, the patron saint of Ireland, to symbolize the three aspects of God, the Trinity. I use it, also symbolically, to make the point that the organization of today is made up of three very different groups of people, groups with different expectations, managed differently, paid differently, organized differently. The key differences were outlined earlier in the book but they need now to be described in more detail with all their implications, not least because each one of us must decide which leaf of the shamrock is for us.

The first leaf of the shamrock represents the core workers, what I prefer to call the professional core because it is increasingly made up of qualified professionals, technicians and managers. These are the people who are essential to the organization. Between them they own the organizational knowledge which distinguishes that organization from its counterparts. Lose them and you lose some of yourself. They are, therefore, precious or should be, and hard to replace. Organizations increasingly bind them to themselves with hoops of gold, with high salaries, fringe benefits and German cars. In return the organization demands of them hard work and long hours, commitment and flexibility. Not for these people are there still 40-hour weeks and 45-week years – few take all their holiday entitlements, few see their houses or their families in daylight. They are expected to go there, do this, be that, as the organization requires. In return they are increasingly well-paid.

As a consequence they are expensive, and as a further consequence there are fewer of them. Every successful organization will tell you that they have at least quadrupled their turnover in the last ten years but have halved their professional core. In three years, from 1982 to 1985, General Electric in the USA reduced its total workforce of 400,000 by 100,000 and its turnover rose. The people who left were mostly staffers, not factory-floor workers and were, apparently, just not necessary; they were expensive luxuries, desirable no doubt but dispensable.

They call it downsizing in the USA, or de-scaling or just re-structuring. The results are the same whatever the language. A Conference Board study in 1987 concluded that since 1979 more than a million managers and staff professionals in the USA had lost their jobs, over half of them since 1983. Many of them were, as one CEO observed, people hired just to read reports which others of them had been hired to write.

If the core is smaller, who then does the work? Increasingly, it is contracted out. It is not sensible, after all, to pay premium rates and give premium conditions to people whose work is not crucial to the organization. The old philosophy of a single-status company in which the cleaners were in principle treated to the same conditions as the directors meant that either you had rather expensive cleaners or rather cheap directors. That had to change as the directors were treated better, or the organization would go bankrupt. All non-essential work, work which could be done by someone else, is therefore sensibly contracted out to people who make a speciality of it and who should, in theory, be able to do it better for less cost. Manufacturing firms are now almost totally assembly firms, while many service organizations are, in effect, brokers, connecting the customer with a supplier with some intervening advice.

Calculations by some organizations revealed that if they broke down all the elements of their product or service, 80 per cent of the value was actually carried out by people not inside their organization. These 20/80 organizations do not always realize how large the contractual fringe has grown because it has become a way of their life. It is only recently that more individual professionals, more small businesses, more hived-off management buy-outs have shone a spotlight on a way of organizing which has, in fact, always existed. It can get exotic: smart Londoners can now get their typing done more cheaply and as quickly in Taiwan as in London using the new communications technology, while the New York Insurance Company has located its New Jersey claims office in Castleisland in Co. Kerry, Ireland, where the people are clever but also cheaper than in New Jersey.

Japan's export organizations have long depended for their efficiency on a large contractual fringe. Just-In-Time delivery means that the subcontractor carries the cost of any stocks. Subcontracts mean that the contractor carries the burden of any slowdown. It is a way of exporting uncertainty. Hence it is that only some 20 per cent of Japanese workers have the security of lifetime employment for they form the central cores of the large organizations. They are crucial, they are special, they are preferentially treated.

The *third* leaf of the shamrock is the flexible labour force, all those part-time workers and temporary workers who are the fastest growing part of the employment scene. That growth is partly a function of the switch to services, for the service industry cannot stockpile its products as a factory does. Some try to do it by putting their customers into a queue, but the more efficient and effective will always try to expand and contract their service to match the requirements of their customers. That means longer opening hours in the retail trade, it means peaks and troughs in demand. Shops now stay open for up to 70 hours a week. Airlines and airports are busier in the summer. Garden centres thrive at weekends. Of course, the full-time core staff could be asked to work the extra hours, or enough people could be employed full-time to cope with any peak and left underemployed the rest of the time. In years gone by both methods were used for they made it more convenient, easier to manage; but, today, the costs would be horrendous, given the increasingly privileged pay and conditions paid to the full-time core. It is cheaper by far, although more trouble, to bring in occasional extra labour part-time, to cope with extra hours, or temporary, to cope with peak periods. Convenience for the management has been weighed against economy and economy has won.

The Discontinuity

The three-leaved workforce has always existed in embryo. What is different today is the scale. *Each* of the leaves is now significant. It happened because it had to. The bad years of the late 1970s and early 1980s forced organizations to make significant reductions in their man-power, most of whom were still full-time employees. The threat of economic disaster forced them, in other words, to cut back their cores. When times improved managers were not going to be caught the same way twice; they did not expand the core but went instead to the other two leaves.

It makes good economic sense, but it also makes life more difficult for those who have to run the organization. Instead of one workforce there are now three, each with a different kind of commitment to the organization, a different contractual arrangement, a different set of expectations. They each have to be managed in different ways.

The core

Increasingly, the core will be composed of well-qualified people, professionals or technicians or managers. They get most of their identity and purpose from their work. They *are* the organization and are likely to be both committed to it and dependent on it. They will work long and hard, but in return they want not only proper rewards in the present but some guarantee of their future. They think in terms of careers, of advancement and of investing in the future. These, then, are not people to be ordered around. These are the new professionals who want their names to be as well-known as their roles, who want to be asked not told to do something, who see themselves in some sense as partners in the enterprise and want to be recognized as colleagues not subordinates.

Life in the core of more and more organizations is going to resemble that of consultancy firms, advertising agencies, and professional partnerships. The organizations are flat, seldom with more than four layers of rank, the top one being the assembly of partners, professors or directors. Promotion through the ranks comes quickly if you are any good (anyone of ability expects to be a partner before 40). Promotion, therefore, soon becomes an inadequate way of rewarding and recognizing people; success for those in the top rank can only mean doing the same job better and, presumably, for more money. At this level, therefore, much of the employee's pay is based on the results of the organization, the employee is in fact if not in law a 'partner'. The Japanese core will commonly take 40 per cent of their total pay in performance-related bonuses. It is the same for all top businessmen. It will soon be the same for most people in the core. It has to be.

This is because no organization can any longer guarantee that this year's pay rise can be next year's base line, not in a time of discontinuity. Therefore, this year's money has to be partly conditioned on this year's results, and next year's on next year's. With smaller cores it will no longer be possible to go in for the five-yearly cull of staff which was for many British organizations the way of reducing labour costs and counteracting the ratchet effect of the annual increment for everyone. Economic necessity, therefore, will force more organizations to re-think the way they reward their senior core people, turning them in the process into partners rather than employees, colleagues rather than bosses and subordinates, names not roles.

The contractual fringe
This is made up of both individuals and organizations. These organizations, although often smaller than the main organization, will have their own shamrocks, their own cores and their own subcontractors. It is a Chinese box type of world. The individuals will be self-employed professionals or technicians, many of them past employees of the central organization who ran out of roles in the core or who preferred the freedom of self-employment.

Whether it be organizations or individuals, however, the organizational principle remains the same – they are paid for results not for time, in fees not wages. The implications of this are important – it means that the central organization can exercise control only by specifying the results, not by overseeing the methods. If that sounds obvious and elementary it also marks a revolution in the way most managers are used to managing. 'Control the means and the methods,' the maxim used to be, 'and the results will be as they should be', or 'If they do what they should, you'll get what you want.' Of course, a proper specification of the results required does involve some investigation of the method proposed but in the end the purchaser can only accept or reject the proffered goods or services.

The management of subcontracting is well-understood in certain industries, particularly those of construction and manufacturing consumer goods. It is less well-understood elsewhere but it needs to be better appreciated.

An organization negotiated to buy back half of the work of one of their staff officers who had decided to go independent. He was their public relations adviser when they decided that they could not afford someone full-time in this role. What they meant but did not say was that they wanted to buy half his time, what they *said* was half his work. They could not control his time since he now worked from his own office and they failed, and did not try, to specify the results they expected. They felt he was now unmanageable, he felt unappreciated. They ended the contract and engaged a different full-time adviser. We often find it easier to manage someone's time than their results, but the contractual fringe does not allow us that luxury.

There are, however, opportunities as well as challenges in the contractual fringe. Fees, for example, make boring work more tolerable, and let us not deceive ourselves, much of the work in organizations *is* boring. I remember how, as a young student, I earned my extra money by printing Christmas cards and stationery on a hand-operated printing machine. There is, I can assure anyone, nothing more monotonous than taking a piece of paper, placing it in the press, pushing down the handle, taking out the paper and placing it on a pile of completed cards, and then repeating the operation 500 times in an hour. Were I doing it for a wage I would have found any excuse to break the routine; a strike, even if doomed to failure, would at least have been a change. But because each printed page placed on the pile represented another few cents of riches I found it a most tolerable form of labour. The result of my effort was immediately visible, and directly rewarded.

The shamrock organization, if it is wise, puts boring work out on contract, paying fees for results. It is piecework rediscovered, but piecework more effective than it used to be because it is no longer a dubious substitute for wages. It is also piecework made more tolerable by better equipment; one man or one woman with good machinery can now do what it once needed a group to do, making the reward more directly proportionate to the individual effort. My printing press today would be automatic, the tedium less and the quality better.

The temptation is to exploit the monopoly power of the organization, to pay minimal fees for maximum output. The challenge is to resist that temptation and to pay good fees for good work. The chamrock organization has to remember that in the contractual fringe it is money paid for work done. There is no longer a residual loyalty to be relied on, no longer any implied promise of security in return for obedient labour. Good work must, in the long run, receive good rewards or it will cease to be good work. The contract is now more explicit, and in many respects more healthy for that.

The flexible labour force
The third leaf of the shamrock is too easily seen as the hired help division, people of whom little is expected and to whom little is given. In crude terms, these people are the labour market, a market into which employers dip as they like and when they need, for as little money as they have to pay. This is a shortsighted philosophy. These people are not all pining for core jobs, marking time on the fringe, having to eke out an existence from part-time earnings until something better turns up. A lot of them are women who do not always want a demanding full-time job, but do want access to money and people, a job to supplement and to complement their other work. Many others have two or more part-time jobs, officially declared, and are therefore more properly described as full-time self-employed with a portfolio of jobs. Some of them are young, who see work as a series of apprenticeships or as pocket money opportunities.

Such people should be taken seriously because for them part-time or temporary work is a choice not just a necessity. They have skills which can be developed, commitment to give, talents and energies to offer if they are required. They do not necessarily hanker after careers or promotion, they have interests and concerns beyond the job and are not therefore susceptible to the same kinds of blandishment as the people of the core. Their commitment will be to a job and to a work group rather than to a career, or to the organization.

Treated as casual labour such people respond casually. A department store that used part-timers to staff their store on Fridays and Saturdays found that their hallowed tradition of service and politeness was visibly dented. They had not invested enough time in training these new staff, nor in persuading them of their ways, because, as they saw it, there was no guarantee that these people would be around long enough to pay back the investment through improved behaviour or better work. That way lies a self-fulfilling prophecy of the worst sort.

Organizations have to get used to the idea that not everyone wants to work for them all the time even if the jobs are available. The ways of the core cannot be and should not be the ways of the flexible labour force, for while some may hanker after full-time lifetime jobs, many will not. The new paradigm of work has begun to take hold of people's minds.

If the flexible labour force is seen to be a valuable part of the organization then the organization will be prepared to invest in them, to provide training, even training leading to qualifications, to give them some status and some privileges (including paid holidays and sick leave entitlement). Then, and only then, will the organization get the temporary or part-time help that it needs to the standard it requires.

The flexible labour force will never, however, have the commitment or the ambition of the core. Decent pay and decent conditions are what they want, fair treatment and good companions. They have jobs not careers and cannot be expected to rejoice in the organization's triumphs any more than they can expect to share in the proceeds, nor will they put themselves out for the love of it; more work, in their culture, deserves and demands more money. It is contract labour but the contract should be fair and must be honoured.

The Fourth Leaf?

There is one other category of sub-contracting which needs to be mentioned. It is the growing practice of getting the customer to do the work. Customers, however, are not paid by the organization so this fourth leaf cannot exist as part of the formal structure of the shamrock (which is just as well for the imagery since no shamrock has four leaves), but it is real all the same.

We now collect our own groceries from the shelves where my parents had shop assistants to do it for them. Our own private cars have replaced the delivery vans. Furniture makers persuade us that it is clever to assemble our own kitchens. Banks long ago worked out that if they could persuade customers to fill in their own deposit slips they, the banks not the customers, would save millions. Now we also draw out our own money from their holes in the wall and call it our convenience. We also pour our own petrol and print out our own tube tickets.

Smart restaurants may one day charge customers for cooking their own food where now they only, in fast food outlets, ask them to clear their own litter, or preferably, take it away and provide their own eating space. 'Help yourself' in clothes stores, supermarkets' pick and mix outlets, drug stores and wine shops has turned out to be a clever way of saving labour under the label of customer preference.

What is clever is that having removed the service, one can then charge extra for providing it as an optional extra, with special delivery or special fitting, or with delicatessens offering the service my parents used to take for granted but now at a premium price. It is all a way of saving labour in the core of the shamrock and reintroducing it as part of the contractual fringe. Clever.

An Interlude

At this point let me pause. Some may well be thinking – yes, I see the sense of what you're saying but is it really happening today? As one manager said to me last month, 'Who *are* all these people you call the self-employed knowledge workers – I don't see any of them on the 8.10 from Woking every morning.' No, said I, you wouldn't. These people don't need to take your trains. They have their terminals and their telephones instead. Sometimes we are so absorbed in our own surroundings that we forget to look over the fence.

This self-absorption happened to me not so long ago. When I need to compose my thoughts and write I go off to a small cottage set amid the fields of East Anglia, not a house in sight. There I can retreat to the peace of a world where nothing ever changes save the seasons. The farm in front is worked by Charlie and Jim, now into their eighties. They still pull the beet by hand for their cattle and slice off the leaves with a sickle as it used to be done 100 years ago. Jim passed by as I was writing.

'Down here for a bit of a holiday, are you?' he said.

'No, I'm working,' I replied, pointing to my papers.

'I'd call that scribbling,' he said with his gentle smile, 'not working.'

Of course, I reflected, the sons of toil have never respected the lily-white hands of the knowledge worker nor known many of them but they say that half the cottages down the lane are now owned by journalists. Perhaps things *are* changing even here. Then I reflected that until two years ago Jim used to clear his ditches with a scythe. Now young Stephen does it for him, for a fee, with his £20,000 Caterpillar digger, wearing ear muffs with walkman earphones stuffed inside – music while you work in the contractual fringe! Quite a skilled contractual fringe, too. Stephen does his own repair work and is starting a business in spare parts on the side.

Charlie grumbles about farm prices. The land is fen land, they can't grow much on it – 'I guess one day it will just go back to fen,' he says. Yet right next door, on land that 40 years ago was sold as gentlemen's rough shooting, is the biggest plant and conifer farm in Britain, indeed in Europe, plants which only need an inch or two of damp soil. Ironically they employ 200 people on 200 acres where Jim and Charlie employ no one, but then those 200 people are quite knowledgeable, at least about their plants and their cultivation. They've done what British manufacturing needs to do everywhere, change the product to a high value-added one that is knowledge-intensive and backed by research and development and in the leisure market, supporting Jonathan Gershuny's point that one person's free time is another person's job. 'That's not farming,' says Jim, 'that's gardening,' and, indeed, I would much prefer to look out at a field of ripening corn than on rows and rows of little conifers, but you don't grow rich on nostalgia.

I tell this little parable to make one point. Until we look around us with fresh eyes we often don't notice what should be obvious. There were the knowledge workers, the highly capitalized contractual workers, the move to a knowledge industry in a spot which I thought was the unchanging heart of rural England. Open your eyes and ye shall see!

Telecommuting

F International in Britain is an electronic shamrock. Francis Kinsman describes it well in his book *The Telecommuters*. It was started by Stephanie (Steve) Shirley in 1962 as a tiny business called Freelance Programmers to be run by her from her own home, writing computer programs for companies. By 1964 it was F International with four other workers and by 1988 it was the F.I. Group plc with 1,100 workers and a turnover of nearly £20 million.

The point about F International, however, is that 70 per cent of those workers work from home or from a local work centre and that over 90 per cent of them are women. F International believes that the performance of their people is 30 per cent higher than their counterparts working in offices where coffee breaks, lunches, corridor gossiping and personal phone calls tend to cut into the working day.

These women are mostly self-employed although, if they can guarantee to commit enough time to the company, they can go on the part-time or even full-time payroll; less than 200 were on salary in 1988. There is a small core staff in the Head Office, a number of small branch offices and, lately, a growing network of work centres where people can take their work if they need to meet with colleagues or to use more specialist equipment. The individual worker is linked into the organization by an electronic mail service, by a newsletter and by free-speaks, in which senior members of the core travel around the country to hold open question and answer sessions.

The women, and some men, in F International are a network built around a core, connected by telephones and computers, working from home rather than at home. They do not work alone but in shifting teams and groups built around specific projects and assignments. It is all designed, as FI's Charter puts it, 'to develop, through modern telecommunications, the unutilized intellectual energy of individuals and groups unable to work in a conventional environment'.

F International is unusual because of Steve Shirley's deliberate plan to create a culture built around the status and talents of independent people. The core grew out of the contractual fringe rather than the other way around. As a result F International invests a lot of time and energy in training its self-employed workers and in keeping in contact with them. It also pays them well.

There aren't many F Internationals around but they are an extreme example of a growing trend. Rank Xerox in Britain has its 'networkers', a group of some 60 or so specialists in marketing, finance, personnel and management services who were peeled off from the central organization and were encouraged to set up their own businesses and sell back some of their services to the parent company. ICL has two groups of high-grade part-timers (as opposed to self-employed) who are software planners and analysts and, as in F International, mainly women with young families.

These, again, are the biggest and most formal examples. It need not, however, be that organized for it to happen. There will hardly be an organization which does not get some of its typing done by someone at home, hardly an executive who has not stayed at home to work on a critical report and called in by telephone to the office. Alvin Toffler in *The Third Wave* quoted a number of eminent Company Presidents in the USA who maintain that between 25 and 75 per cent of what they do could be done at home or from home once the necessary communications are in place. Francis Kinsman quotes examples from the American companies of organized homeworker schemes, of which Freight Data systems in California is the most interesting. They let their small staff work at home when they were not needed in the office, but encouraged them to work ahead of time by means of a bonus system. They increased productivity so much that it paid for the capital cost of a terminal in each home inside five months, and the rapid growth of the company caused them no space problems and no need to move to bigger and more costly premises.

What, one might ask, is so unusual about all this, except for the electronic gadgetry? Publishers, after all, rely on authors scribbling at home for their new material. Home-workers have knitted sweaters, addressed envelopes, marked examination papers, typed scripts, cooked pies and made quilts for centuries. The Japanese have always relied on a cottage industry tradition of small manufacturers and assemblers as the raft on which to build their huge enterprises. What is new is the higher skills, qualifications and status of the new homeworkers. The Department of Employment in Britain discovered in 1987, probably to its surprise, that some of the highest paid workers worked at home. The rate for one fifth of all the homeworkers in their survey put them in the top 10 per cent of all earnings. Homeworkers are out, telecommuters are in. It's all in the language but it is the language which signals the change, the change from freak to fashion.

Telecommuters have choice; they can choose to work before the commuter trains start running or when offices are long closed. They can commute by telephone or computer link from wherever, can move house without moving job, can revel in the occasional hour of sunshine or take time off to celebrate an anniversary with no one's permission to obtain; they can work fast or work slowly, by the fire or in the attic. It is not, however, to everyone's taste. For some it is too lonely, or the temptations of home become too great; one American lady complained that she put on two stone because of frequent trips to the fridge, and one man attributed his divorce to the fact that he was at home all the time.

Yet what today seems yuppie and freaky may be tomorrow's commonplace. The telephone has turned out to be the most user-friendly of all modern inventions and as its permutations and ramifications extend it will start to revolutionize ordinary occupations. The carphone and the cordless telephone have surprised even the most optimistic of manufacturers by their popularity. The fax is bringing handwriting back into fashion as we find that we can instantaneously reproduce our scribbled notes or diagrams half a world away. The computer and its screen, linked to a telephone cable, becomes a message box for the world, one which your local store can use to sell its wares, your friends to leave their calls, your business its memos, and now that we call it keyboard skills rather than typing (new words again!) everybody can learn to use it without loss of face or dignity.

In September 1988 the Confederation of British Industry organized a huge conference in London on 'teleworking' along with British Telecom, to celebrate an 'idea whose time has come', to quote Francis Kinsman and in recognition of their estimate that by 1995 there will be 4 million tele-workers in Britain. Four million people cannot escape notice even if they are working from home. The world is changing.

The Club Centre

One sign of the electronic shamrock will be a new concept of the central office. At present the office is an apartment house, a collection of private apartments for executives with all the attendant service functions. It is an expensive way of accommodating the work, something that became very obvious on a recent visit to one such office in central London. The chief executive was thinking of re-designing the floor layout to allow, he said, for more informal interaction between his executives, for more meeting rooms and rooms dedicated to particularly expensive pieces of electronic hardware. He showed me round to point out the disadvantages of the present layout of rooms as rows, or rather layers and layers (for it was a tall narrow building) of individual offices.

'But they are all empty,' I exclaimed.

'Of course,' he replied, 'they are all out doing business, seeing clients, attending meetings, gathering information, making deals. They only come in here to file their reports, attend departmental meetings or deal with their correspondence.

'Costed per hour of occupancy,' I said, 'you must have the most expensive rooms in London. You ought to see my friend Walter.'

'Why?' he asked, not unnaturally.

'Walter,' I explained, 'runs a design and consultancy business with a staff of around 100 professionals – quite big. He runs it from a converted warehouse, except that he hasn't converted it very much. There are no offices in it. There are meeting rooms, there is a superb farmhouse kitchen, there are drawing-boards scattered around, there are word-processors, telephones and computers abounding but no one, not even Walter himself, has any private space – except for the secretaries, who are really not secretaries as such but project co-ordinators, each assigned to work for a project rather than for an individual.'

When I asked him why he'd done this, Walter told me, 'I don't want my designers and consultants spending their time here in this very expensive space. I would rather they were out with the client or working at home where I will provide any equipment they want. They only come in here for meetings, to use some specialist equipment and, generally, to keep in touch. We lay on the best breakfasts in town in that kitchen of ours and there's always a bottle of wine open and waiting for anyone dropping in after 6.00 pm. It's a working club really.'

Indeed it was, a working club, a club being a place of privileged access to common facilities. A club not an apartment house. Turning the office into a club allows one to equip it far more lavishly and comfortably than a set of individual offices and to make sure that all the space is properly used. The idea of a club centre only works, however, if people have somewhere else to be, at home, with clients, out on business. It is the perfect facility for a network of individuals linked into a small core (in Walter's case the core was primarily the project co-ordinators).

F International, interestingly, is creating a number of regional work centres, places where their individual workers can go when they need to attend team meetings, use more specialist equipment or just want to escape from their homes and meet people. The work centres are working clubs and we shall see more of them because they are cost effective.

The shamrock organization, always there in embryo, has flourished because organizations have realized that you do not have to employ all of the people all of the time to get the work done. They are now going further and are counting the cost of having all of them around in the same place for all of the time. Offices for part-timers become common-rooms for telecommuters and, in time, clubs for everyone. The early morning crush in the commuter train will one day be a thing of the past or at least only a twice-weekly chore.

Homeworking is not, traditionally, good working – particularly for women. Men have in the past had the fun jobs, going out to work. For women, the paid work at home has been lonely, monotonous, trivial and badly paid. More homeworking, even glamorized by words like telecommuting, would not therefore seem to be good news. Times, however, may be changing.

Catherine Hakim, in Britain, has done an extensive analysis of homeworkers in Britain in 1981 for the Department of Employment. Even in 1981, she reports, the usual picture of homeworking – of work typically done by women, tied to the home with few or no skills, exploited and in poor health – was highly misleading and only applied to the small percentage doing manufacturing homework.

Her survey concluded that homeworkers are more highly qualified than most, in better health than most, and more likely to own their own homes. Many of the women in the survey were making conscious trade-offs between the flexibility of homework and the relatively low-paid job available, which probably explains why the majority of homeworkers say they are satisfied with their pay and conditions.

On the other hand, Barbara Baran in the United States studied women's work in the insurance industry and concluded that although the new technologies may be freeing women from the pink-collar assembly lines and even raising skill levels of the female workforce, there is, in the end, she says 'little cause for good cheer'. For women at the bottom end of the clerical hierarchy, jobs are simply disappearing. For skilled and particularly white clericals there will be jobs but not career opportunities. In one company one sixth of their clerical staff (mostly women) were working from home. Numbers of college-educated women may make their way into professional and managerial ranks only to find their talents, she says, under-utilized and undervalued.

Yet she also reports from companies in her study who had moved their operations from major cities to adjacent suburban areas in search of a higher quality clerical workforce – the labour pool of educated women with small children. Automation, she was told, is raising skill requirements and forcing insurance companies to relocate to be nearer high quality labour. Perhaps not all women want to be career professionals like men. If they don't then homeworking may be good news, with new types of work and new technology.

The Challenges Of The Shamrock

On the face of it the shamrock organization is logical. Logic, however, does not necessarily imply ease and these are not easy organizations to run. Meetings, planned or ad hoc, teams and committees are a familiar feature of organizations and they survive and flourish in the core, but to try to fix a quick meeting with members of the contractual fringe is a recipe for frustration and disappointment for these are the meetings that have to be negotiated weeks in advance with great comparing of diaries, inevitable absentees and compromises. Each leaf of the shamrock has to be managed differently and must yet be somehow part of the whole. The shamrock, after all, symbolizes three different aspects of one whole, three in one and one in three.

Accepting and recognizing the need for differences is only the start. The most difficult of policy decisions concerns what and who belongs in the core, what activities and which people. Too often organizations drift into this decision, gradually hiving off functions until they are left with what is inconceivable or too inconvenient to give to others. It is not an obvious choice; most organizations, if they start thinking radically enough, can justify out-sourcing, to use the current jargon, almost anything. In one organization such a brain storming exercise left only the chief executive and a car phone! A growing subsidiary business today is dedicated to answering customer complaints – on behalf of other businesses! It is a service which big companies contract out, wisely or not, getting a periodic analysis of the complaints as part of the deal.

Even more contentious can be the question of *who* belongs in the core and for how long. Smaller, flatter, more intense organizations tend to be younger. The older men cannot always stand the pace, can get out-of-date in some technologies, or become, in general, too expensive for the value which they add. The fixed-term contracts of the armed services will increasingly be a feature of the new cores. As we shall see in Chapter 6, the task of keeping the core people up-to-date and mentally alert and open is one of increasing importance to all organizations. Fewer people means better people; there is no room now for incompetence or passengers in today's cores. This pressure for quality in turn means greater selectivity on entry. More will be demanded of the aspiring executive, with more organizations tempted towards the ultimate Catch 22 of employment – 'We won't hire you unless you have previous successful experience in this area'. Rather like an actor in pursuit of an Equity card without which no acting job is possible but which you cannot apply for without an acting job, it is hard today to know where to begin.

The core is the critical hub of an organizational network. It is essential to get it right and to manage it right.

5 The Federal Organization

Alongside the emerging shamrock organization we can discern the gradual development of the federal organization. Federalism implies a variety of individual groups allied together under a common flag with some shared identity. Federalism seeks to make it big by keeping it small, or at least independent, by combining autonomy with co-operation. It is the method which businesses are slowly, and painfully, evolving for getting the best of both worlds - the size which gives them clout in the market-place and in the financial centres, as well as some economies of scale, and the small unit size which gives them the flexibility which they need, as well as the sense of community for which individuals increasingly hanker.

The Nature of Federalism

Federalism is *not* a classy word for decentralization. The differences are important and are too little understood by monarchical countries like Britain which has always regarded federalism as something more appropriate for departing colonies or vanquished enemies because, presumably, it would keep them divided and therefore weak, in spite of much historical evidence that it tends to do exactly the opposite.

Decentralization implies that the centre delegates certain tasks or duties to the outlying bits while the centre remains in overall control. The centre does the delegating, and initiates and directs. Thus it is that we have that most

consistent of organizational findings, the more an organization decentralizes its operations the greater the flow of
information to and from the centre. The centre may not be
doing the work in a decentralized organization, but it makes
sure that it knows how the work is going. The new
technology, of course, makes it even easier for that information to flow more copiously and more immediately than
ever, making it ever easier to contemplate still further
decentralization, in theory at least.

Federalism is different. In federal countries states are the
original founding groups, coming together because there
are some things which they can do better jointly (defence is
the obvious example) than individually. The centre's powers
are given to it by the outlying groups, in a sort of reverse
delegation. The centre, therefore, does not direct or control
so much as co-ordinate, advise, influence and suggest – all
words which are familiar currency in the Head Offices of
multinationals, multinationals who have often been forced
into federalism because of the local priorities of their
subsidiaries.

Federal organizations, therefore, are reverse thrust
organizations; the initiative, the drive and the energy comes
mostly from the bits, with the centre an influencing force,
relatively low in profile. Switzerland is a good example of
the federal principle at work, a country both peaceful and
prosperous, in many ways the envy of its European
neighbours. Surely, one would have thought, her government would be much admired, her President's name on
every lip. It is instead ironic that even when he is host to a
summit conference no one readily remembers who he is, or,
to be precise, who he was, because the job rotates. It is seen
as a chairman's role, the chairman of a co-ordinating group
who seek to guide but not direct the nation's affairs,
important but low in profile.

Federal organizations are, as a result, tight-loose organizations, to use the management jargon. The centre holds

some decisions very tight to itself, usually, and crucially, the choice of how to spend new money and where and when to place new people. This gives them the means to shape the long-term strategy and to influence its execution through the key executives. It is a way of working long familiar to other institutions. I once asked the Headmaster of one of England's more famous independent schools how he changed the place. 'I choose the new heads of houses and heads of departments; I allocate resources to some new facilities, he said, and then I wait ten years for the results.'

Federalism, however, is not a free or willing choice for most organizations. There is, as far as I know, no example in history of any state voluntarily ceding power from the centre to its component parts. Federal constitutions arise when individual states decide to merge together, as in Australia, or when the central power is destroyed by war or revolution, as in West Germany, and no one, inside or out, wants to see so much power in the centre again.

How then, one must ask, has federalism come to organizations? Not willingly, nor in most cases deliberately or even consciously. Once again this significant piece of discontinuity has crept up on us unawares. It has happened perforce because the reduced core of the organization cannot deal with the flood of information coming in from the decentralized operations. As the shamrock took shape, as a bigger organization grew more and smaller shamrocks it tried to run them all from the core at the centre, relying on the new technologies to provide all the information needed. The new technologies did not fail, but information, to be useful, still has to be interpreted by its human masters. More information with more diversity needs more people to interpret it if it is not to lie unused in the piles of printout or in the unseen memories of the computers. Yet, paradoxically, organizations were all, as we have seen, seeking to contract their cores and cut down their staffers. In the end they have to stop asking for the information, have to stop trying to run everything from the centre, have to begin to let go. Then it is that decentralization turns into federalism, a discontinuity whose significance is not understood and not therefore developed by many a chief executive.

'How many hundreds of people do you have in that Head Office of yours?' I asked a friend of mine, a newly appointed Chief Executive of a multinational who had asked me to explain federalism. 'Fifteen, I think,' he said. 'There you are,' I said, slightly triumphantly, 'the point about federalism is small centres, with the other parts doing the real work. With federal thinking you would not need fifteen hundred people cluttering up London's airspace.'

'I said fifteen,' he replied, 'not fifteen hundred. You see,' he explained indulgently, 'all my operations are done by independent companies. At the centre we collect their surpluses and invest them in new opportunities and we watch them to see that they are producing the surpluses we think they should. If they don't we push the top people a bit and ultimately replace them. New ventures and new people, that's my concern in the centre and I only need a few wise and a few clever people to help me.'

'You don't need me,' I said, 'you have discovered organizational federalism all by yourself.'

'I would call it commonsense,' he replied.

Fifteen people cannot even begin to think of controlling in any detail the operations of perhaps thirty different companies, divisions or operating units; they would not have time to even read the information which might be available. It is better in the end that they do not even try, but concentrate instead on the things they can control and the decisions which they alone should take. Small cores make federalism ultimately inevitable and large cores make decentralization ultimately too expensive. The slow imperative of economical reality pushes larger organizations into a new kind of world.

The Role Of The Centre

A report for Britain's National Economic Development Office in 1988 was severely critical of some of the country's largest electronic businesses. They had, said the report, been growing depressingly slowly compared with their competitors in Japan, Germany and the USA. The report suggested that a major cause of this slow growth lay in the corporate structure adopted by these companies. They had broken themselves down into individual businesses and had then left those businesses to determine their own strategies. The result, too often, was short-term and parochial thinking. The implication was that it needs big organizations to think big and long-term.

If these companies had indeed devolved strategic thinking to their individual businesses then they had misunderstood corporate federalism. It would be akin to the USA letting the States decide on their individual policies for defence - no one would, in the end, be defending the USA. To see the centre only as a banker, pulling in surplus profits and dispensing funds for worthwhile projects, is to throw away most of the advantages of federalism which is a concept devised to make things big whilst keeping them small.

The centre has to be more than a banker. Only the centre can think beyond the next annual report or indeed, to quote one family business, can look beyond the grave. Only the centre can think in terms of global strategies which may link one or more of the autonomous parts. To leave these big decisions to the discretion of the parts can be a way to mortgage the future.

The centre, however, is not in full control in a federal organization. It is easy, in logic, to think of the centre taking the long-term decisions and leaving the implementation to the parts. That logic, however, reeks of the old engineering language of management, of decentralization and of delegated tasks and controls. It is not the new language of political theory, of people and communities. The federal concept requires the centre to act on behalf of the parts, if the resulting decisions are going to be self-enforcing – and they have to be because the centre does not have the manpower to control the detail.

It all requires a new image of the corporation, one in which the centre genuinely is at the middle of things and is not a polite word for the top, or even for Head Office (a term gradually disappearing from the corporate vocabulary). The centre must cling to its key functions of new people and new money, but its decisions have to be in consultation with, and on behalf of, the chiefs of the parts. In political terms this makes sense – the centre becomes an assembly of chiefs, acting in that place and time on behalf of the total federation, then returning to their own tribes to do their own bit for the whole.

Running the federal centre is not therefore the job for a monarch, someone with an overarching authority and a liking for autocratic government. It has to be a place of persuasion, of argument leading to consensus. Leadership is required but it is the leadership of ideas not of personality. It is observable how the bigger multinationals, pushed earlier than most into federalism because they have to deal with autonomous nation states, have begun to create triumvirates, even committees, to run the centre.

I asked someone who had just become Chairman of a great multinational what it felt like to be head of one of the world's biggest businesses, to be, in one sense, one of our biggest businessmen. 'It isn't like that,' he replied. 'I have just moved round the table and I'm temporarily chairing the team because someone has to.'

In 1984 Noburo Goto, the charismatic head of the Tokyo group in Japan, with 300 companies ranging from railways to property, resigned and in his place the company is run by a group. From monarchy to federalism in one move.

The centre will have its own staff in these organizations,

a staff whose concerns will largely be with the future, with plans and possibilities, scenarios and options. They will be there to advise their political seniors, many of whom will be in the part not the centre, and will have to rely increasingly on influence rather than on any formal authority or absolute power. In many organizations the centre is already becoming a training place for future chiefs, a necessary exposure to the whole before a commitment to one of the parts.

As these organizations evolve there are, as yet, few federal corporations in a pure form. The Japanese have always come close to it and, more recently, Isamu Yamashita of Mitsui was quoted (in John Naisbitt's *Reinventing the Corporation*) as saying, 'The best corporate structure today comprises a small strategic centre supported by many front-line outfits.' New words, however, are, once again, heralding new behaviours. One chief executive recently described his corporate centre as variously a 'Good Food Guide' (indicating which subsidiaries were best for what), traffic policeman, orchestra conductor, interpreter, critic or cheerleader. Asked about his own role, he replied, 'For most of my life I'm a missionary'. 'We need', he said 'to compete outside but collaborate within', a succinct description of the federal principle of interdependence, the principle that each part needs the help of the other parts, as well as the centre, in order to survive. Too much independence, after all, can lead to breakaway or to a random collection of disparate bits, a conglomerate not a federation.

Unfortunately, federalism misunderstood can be worse than no federalism. Federalism misunderstood becomes inefficient decentralization, leading to talk of the headless corporation or the hollow company and the kinds of criticisms cited in the NEDO Report of Britain's electronic businesses. A clear understanding of the role of the centre is crucial to a proper federalism, but so is an appreciation of concepts like 'subsidiarity' and 'the inverted do'nut' because structure on its own will not produce a federalist organization. The words are deliberately strange to signal that new ways of thinking are required in these organizations. More of the same will no longer work. Discontinuity demands upside-down thinking.

Subsidiarity

The federal organization is not only different in its form and shape, it is culturally different, it requires a different set of attitudes from those who seek to run it and from those who seek to manage it and from those who are managed. This is the discontinuity which matters – not the change in structure but the change in philosophy.

That philosophy is characterized by the word 'subsidiarity'. It is a word unfamiliar to most, but not to the adherents of the Roman Catholic Church where it has long been an established part of traditional doctrine. First enunciated by Pope Leo XIII, but later recalled in the papal encyclical 'Quadragesimo Anno' in 1941 at the time of Mussolini, the principal of subsidiarity holds that 'it is an injustice, a grave evil and a disturbance of right order for a large and higher organization to arrogate to itself functions which can be performed efficiently by smaller and lower bodies'. To steal people's decisions is wrong.

The choice of word is deliberate because the sense of morality implied by it is crucial to its working. Subsidiarity means giving away power. No one does that willingly in organizations, yet the federal organization will not work unless those in the centre not only *have* to let go of some of their power but actually *want* to do so, because only then will they trust the new decision-makers to take the right decisions and only then will they enable them to make them work. They have, therefore, to believe that it is an essentially *good* thing to do; they have to feel good in themselves about it because they have done the good thing.

It is only too easy in organizations to create negative self-fulfilling prophecies and to delegate with the secret knowledge that it won't work because the individual to whom you have delegated does not have the right information, or access to it, cannot mobilize the resources to implement any decisions and is inadequately trained for the new responsibilities. It would, of course, be an irresponsible manager who delegated under these circumstances but we can all act irresponsibly when we act reluctantly. To be effective, delegation requires a positive will to trust and to enable and a willingness to be trusted and enabled, a positive self-fulfilling prophecy, a moral act, subsidiarity.

Interestingly, virtue in this instance does not go unrewarded. It is the way out of one of the many Catch 22 situations in organizations. This Catch 22 starts from the observable fact that it is hard to give responsibility to someone if they are not capable of it, but how do you have any evidence of their capability if they have never been given the responsibility? Trust has to be earned, but in order to be earned it has first to be given. I must first trust my children to find their own way to school if I am to find out whether they can be trusted to get there on their own. I will do that because I am their parent, because I want them to grow and because I believe that they are capable, give or take one or two initial mistakes.

Those organizations which are forced, often because of the nature of their work, to give large responsibilities to young and junior people have a very good record of attracting a high calibre of young people, which makes it easier for those above to take the risks implied by subsidiarity. Television and journalism are both arenas which the talented young queue up to join. It cannot be the money, nor is it usually the fame; it is the chance to take responsibility publicly at an early age. It has to work this way because no one in the centre of a television company or a newspaper can specify in any detail what has to go into every programme or every page; those in power have to rely on control after the event, which can at times be embarrassing and even expensive. These are the mistakes which are an inevitable part of trust. In good organizations the mistakes are rare because the people are good, they are good because they know that they will be entrusted with big responsibilities, including the chance to make mistakes.

Practice subsidiarity, in other words, and in due course you will draw unto yourself the kinds of people whom you will need if the subsidiarity is to work. Increasingly we see subsidiarity infecting other areas of work, in the new finance houses, for example, in advertising agencies, in the more traditional fields of medicine and now of law; in places, in other words, where decisions have to move so fast that those on the spot have to be trusted. Where the young perceive it happening is where the best of them want to be. Ultimately subsidiarity is a self-justifying philosophy.

The Inverted Do'nut

An alternative analogy is that of the inverted do'nut. The do'nut is an American doughnut. It is round with a hole in the middle rather than the jam in its British equivalent. Call it a bagel if you live in New York. This, however, is an inverted American do'nut, in that it has the hole in the middle filled in and the space on the outside; like the diagram below:

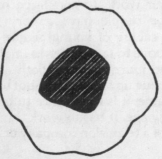

The point of the analogy begins to emerge if you think of your job, of any job. There will be a part of that job which will be clearly defined, and which, if you do not do, you will clearly be seen to have failed. That is the heart, the core, the centre of the do'nut. The tasks may be written down in a job description, or, if it's a classy organization, in a statement of objectives; the snag is that when you have done all that you have not finished, for there is more. In any job of any significance the person holding the job is expected not only to do all that is required but in some way to improve on that, to make a difference, to show responsible and appropriate initiative, to move into the empty space of the do'nut and begin to fill it up. Unfortunately, no one can tell you what you should do there because if they could they would make it part of the core. It is another organizational Catch 22. All they can tell you is the boundary of your discretion, the outer rim of the do'nut.

Some do'nuts are all core and no space. We do not want the bus driver using his initiative to leave early, take a quicker route or go for scenic detours. Some people, particularly perhaps those in the flexible labour force, want jobs which are all core; at least one knows what has to be done and when it is done. Other jobs have no rims, that of the independent entrepreneur, for instance, and some have huge areas of space as with people in the caring professions, teaching or the priesthood, where there always seems to be more that could be done were there only the time. Most people seem to like a balanced do'nut with about equal spaces of core and space.

The point is that federal organizations require large do'nuts, be they group do'nuts or individual do'nuts. That is not as it used to be. Organizational fashion used to imply that the work of most of the organization could be precisely described and defined, and therefore carefully monitored and controlled. Most jobs were all core. The changing complexity, variety and spread of reaction which is now a feature of so many organizations makes the well-cored do'nut an impossible dream today, if dream it ever was. These organizations have to be managed by specifying the essential cores of do'nuts, by being clear about boundaries or areas of discretion, and by specifying the kinds of results which are required from each do'nut, the criteria for successful initiative.

Obvious though it may sound when set down on paper, this philosophy of management marks a major discontinuity. We are not, most of us, used to running organizations by results, with large and empty do'nuts. Most managers feel more comfortable when the cores are large as well as closely defined, when they can control the methods and therefore the results, the means and not the ends. To let go, to specify success criteria, to trust people to use their own methods to achieve your ends – this can be uncomfortable. It is particularly uncomfortable when we realize that after-the-event controls, or management-by-results, means that mistakes can and will be made. It may be true that we learn more from our mistakes than from our successes but organizations have in the past been reluctant to put this theory into practice. Now they will have to, *and* they will have to learn to forgive mistakes. Not all mistakes, of course, can be forgiven but most are less critical than they seem at the time and can be the crux of important lessons.

Organizations are not by nature forgiving places. Mistakes are magnified by myth and engraved in reports and appraisals, to be neither forgotten nor forgiven. Organizational halos are for sinners as well as for saints and last for a long time. The new manager must be a different manager. He, and increasingly she, must use what, in psychological jargon, is called re-inforcement theory, applauding success and forgiving failure; he or she must use mistakes as an opportunity for learning, something only possible if the mistake is *truly* forgiven because otherwise the lesson is heard as a reprimand not an offer of help. The new manager must learn to specify the measures of success as well as the signs of failure and must then allow his or her people the space to get on with it in their own way. The new manager has to be teacher, counsellor and friend, as much as or more than he or she is commander, inspector and judge. It is a major change in our ways of managing. If we cannot do it then federalism becomes anarchy, control reverts to the centre, the centre becomes too big and too expensive, the organization is crippled, withers and can die.

The Language Of Leadership

The new organizations need to be run in new ways. As we have seen, these new ways need a new language to describe them, a language of federations and networks, of alliances and influences, as well as of shamrocks and do'nuts. The language, and the philosophy which it describes, requires us to learn new ways and new habits, to live with more uncertainty but more trust, less control but more creativity. To those of us reared in another tradition it can be a strange and a frightening language but I think that we have to recognize that it is the *right* language. No one, after all, has ever liked being managed, even if they didn't mind being the manager, for anyone who has tried to run an organization has always known that it was more like running a small country than a machine. It was only the theorists who tried to apply the hard rules of number and logic and mechanics to an essentially soft system. Maybe we were instinctively right to pay little heed to them until people like Peters and Waterman first started talking the new language in their *In Search of Excellence*, a book which obviously touched some chord.

As a result, leadership is now fashionable and the language of leadership increasingly important but, as

Warren Bennis says in his book on *Leaders*, it remains the most studied and least understood topic in all the social sciences. Like beauty, or love, we know it when we see it but cannot easily define or produce it on demand. Again, like beauty and love, the writings on it are fun, sexy even, with their pictures of heroes and stories that can be our private fantasies. To read MacGregor Burns, Maccoby, Alistair Mant, Warren Bennis, Cary Cooper or Peters and Waterman themselves is to escape into a private world of might-have-beens.

They may even do a disservice, these fun books, with their tales of heroes and their myths of the mighty, by suggesting that leadership is only for the new and the special. The significance of the new language is, I believe, that leadership has to be endemic in organizations, the fashion not the exception. Everyone with pretensions to be anyone must begin to think and act like a leader. Some will find it comes naturally and will blossom, some will not enjoy it at all, but unless you try, and are allowed to try, no one will ever know, for leadership is hard if not impossible to detect in embryo – it has to be seen in action to be recognized by oneself as much as by others.

So what is this mysterious thing and how does one acquire it? The studies agree on very little but what they do agree on is probably at the heart of things. It is this: 'A leader shapes and shares a vision which gives point to the work of others.' Would that it were as easy to do as to say! Think on these aspects of that short sentence:

— The vision must be different. A plan or a strategy which is a projection of the present or a replica of what everyone else is doing is not a vision. A vision has to 're-frame' the known scene, to re-conceptualize the obvious, connect the previously unconnected dream. Alistair Mant talks of the leader as 'builder' working with others towards a 'third corner', a goal. Those who are interested only in power or achievement for its own sake he calls 'raiders' or mere 'binary' people. MacGregor Burns talks of the 'transforming' leader as opposed to the mere 'transactional' one, the busy fixer.

— The vision must make sense to others. Ideally it should create the 'Aha Effect', which I described earlier, as when everyone says 'Aha – of course, now I see it', like wit perhaps – what often was thought but ne'er so well expressed. To make sense it must stretch people's imaginations but still be within the bounds of possibility. To give point to the work of others it must be related to their work and not to some grand design in which they feel they have no point. If 'vision' is too grand a word, try 'goal' or even 'manifesto'.

— The vision must be understandable. No one can communicate a vision that takes two pages to read, or is too full of numbers and jargon. It has to be a vision that sticks in the head. Metaphor and analogy can be keys because they provide us with vivid images with room for interpretation – low definition concepts as opposed to the more precise high definition words of engineering and management.

— The leader must live the vision. He, or she, must not only believe in it but must be seen to believe in it. It is tempting credulity to proclaim a crusade for the impoverished from a luxury apartment. Effective leaders, we are told, exude energy. Energy comes easily if you love your cause. Effective leaders, again, have integrity. Integrity, being true to yourself, comes naturally if you live for your vision. In other words, the vision cannot be something thought up in the drawing office, to be real it has to come from the deepest parts of you, from an inner system of belief. The total pragmatist cannot be a transforming leader.

— The leader must remember that it is the work of others. The vision remains a dream without that work of others. A leader with no followers is a voice in the wilderness. Leaders like to choose their teams but most inherit them and must then make them their own. Trust in others is repaid by trust from them. If it is to be *their* vision too, then their ideas should be heeded.

These six principles sound simple, obvious even, but in practice they are hard to deliver. Old-fashioned management is easier than the new leadership. Yet, if the new organizations are going to succeed, and they must succeed, our managers must think like leaders. If it happens, and in places it is happening, it will mark yet one more important discontinuity turned to advantage.

Horizontal tracking
How many leaders will one organization need? A lot, must be the answer, lots of them, all over the place and not only in the centre. Federal organizations are flat organizations and the cores of their parts will be four or five levels only.

The consequences are profound. Organizations used to look like a collection of ladders tied together at the top. A career for most people meant climbing the ladders. Success was rewarded by promotion to the next rung. Fast-moving careerists might expect to move up a rung every two years. There were some cross-over points and some general management jobs lower down, but on the whole the analogy holds for the larger organizations of Europe and the USA.

Ladder-thinking could reach bizarre extremes. I once visited an Indian organization which employed 20,000 people in a big shed in the middle of India making turbine generating equipment. The organization was suffering from bureaucratic arthritis. Nothing could be made to happen. Everyone seemed to have a power of veto over every decision. A quick look at the organization chart revealed that there were, on average, twenty rungs in each ladder in the organization, twenty levels of command. 'Well, you see,' they said, 'we are enormously taken with this British idea of an annual appraisal, but good appraisals need to be rewarded with promotion otherwise Indians lose face, therefore we have had to create all these opportunties for promotion within our factory.'

Federal organizations do not put 20,000 people in one shed. Wherever possible it will be less than 500 in each individual part, and the ladders will be short. In the core of the shamrock, as we noted in Chapter 4, success will not, cannot, mean promotion because the layers are not there. There is no god beyond the senior partner and he or she is likely to be in their forties.

What then does a career mean if it isn't always upwards? For some it will be more of the same only better. For others it will be more variety, a different job at the same level. The Japanese have a nice way of developing their high potential young people. They actually have a fast-track route for them, but instead of it being a vertical fast-track up through the organization, it is a horizontal fast-track, a succession of different jobs, real jobs with tough standards to be met, but all at the same level. The advantages are that not only does the young person get a wider view of the organization he or she gets a chance to test out their talents and skills in a wide variety of roles. Few excel at everything. Fortune favours the one who can early in life divine what they are good at. Japanese systems make it more likely that fortune will smile on the many not the few by giving them so many test beds for talents.

What works for the young in Japan can work for all ages everywhere. The horizontal fast-track can apply to seniors as well as to juniors. It is a Western notion that people's abilities and inclinations are formed in their middle to late teens, after which education and experience tend to drive them up one ladder and one ladder only. Too many people discover too late that they picked the wrong ladder. The functional organization, joined to a functional education system, can result in a one-start society. A flatter organization can offer opportunities at all ages to discover new abilities and new interests.

It is upside-down thinking again, of course; horizontal careers as a good thing. To work, it requires that the organization has faith in the ability of its people to learn and to go on learning; and believes, moreover, that learning is not linear, more of the same, but can be lateral and even discontinuous; that people, even in their forties and fifties, may have talents which even they are not aware of; that our past performance is not always the best guide to our future potential if we change our role.

Without such upside-down thinking organizations will find themselves with growing numbers of so-called 'plateaued' managers, managers who have run out of ladder and have nowhere else to go except out; organizations will spend more money and time than they want to on hiring new faces for new boxes; they will worry about the lack of motivation in some of their more senior executives, about the cultural disharmony that comes with the importing of too many new faces and about their inability to offer meaningful careers to their younger people.

Federalism is, in my view, a necessary development in the evolution of organizations. It allows individuals to work in organization villages with the advantages of big city facilities. Organizational cities no longer work unless they are broken down into villages. In their big city mode they cannot cope with the variety needed in their products, their processes and their people. On the other hand, the villages on their own have not the resources nor the imagination to grow. Some villages, of course, will be content to survive, happy in their niche, but global markets need global products and large confederations to make them or do them.

These organizational villages can also be geographical villages. Today, federalism makes it possible to bring the work to the people rather than the people to the work and to link them all together telephonically and electronically instead of in flesh and blood. In the end organizational federalism may well solve the housing problem in Britain.

It requires a little upside-down thinking, to be sure. At present, organizations in the South of Britain, and in the South of other countries too, are short of the workers and the skills they need. There are too many unemployed or underemployed in the North but they cannot afford to move house to the expensive South and, indeed, do not particularly want to. It is better to be poor in the place you know.

Instead of paying even higher salaries to attract them down, thus inflating house prices still further, organizations will increasingly see the wisdom of locating some of their work in the North. Once they realize that if they embrace federalism they do not *all* have to move North, the move will start to happen.

Nor will it just be from North to South. In the new organizations of the information society it is people who are the key assets, particularly the brainy people. Organizations always move close to their key assets or raw materials; when it was coal they went to the coalfields, now they will move to where their people want to live and their key people will often want to live near a university city and pleasant country, where there is good education to be had, good communications and a sense of space. More and more it will pay organizations to move their villages to the villages. Federalism allows them to do so and still be a city themselves.

Federalism is, however, about more than structure, as this chapter has sought to make plain. It involves a change in thinking about people and their capacities, about the way they can be asked to work and the way they are managed. They have in fact to be 'smart' as well as 'federal'. It is this requirement which the next chapter addresses.

6 The Triple I Organization

It was Wally Olins who summed it up for me. A large part of his work, and that of his successful company, involves helping organizations to discover and to express visually their strengths and their purposes. He is, therefore, in an excellent position to observe the way things are changing in organizations, and changing they are. 'Wealth in the past,' he observed, 'used to be based on the ownership of land, then, more recently on the capacity to make things. Increasingly, today, it is based on knowledge and on the ability to use that knowledge.'

The new formula for success, and for effectiveness, is $I^3 = AV$, where I stands for Intelligence, Information and Ideas, and AV means added value in cash or in kind. In a competitive information society brains on their own are not enough, they need good information to work with and ideas to build on if they are going to make value out of knowledge.

We are talking, of course, of the core of organizations, of the heart of the place. There will still be mundane jobs in these organizations; mail has to be opened, visitors looked after, offices cleaned, light bulbs replaced and meetings arranged. These things will never all be automated nor do they need budding geniuses to do them. But unless the heart of the operation is a Triple I concern there will eventually be no added value to pay for the support services.

Triple I organizations are different. Not for them the organizational philosophies of the army, or the factory, or the bureacracies of government. They must look instead to some of the places where knowledge has always been key and brains more important than brawn.

'Increasingly,' I said at a conference of chief executives, 'your corporations will come to resemble universities or colleges.'

'Then God help us all,' one of them replied.

But I was serious, although I went on to agree that universities could with advantage get more like businesses.

Universities or colleges, my point was, are places where intelligent people are concerned with information and with ideas, the triple i. They use these three i's, in theory at least, to pursue truth in an atmosphere of learning

The new organization, making added value out of knowledge, needs also to be obsessed with the pursuit of truth or, in business language, of quality. To that end the wise organization increasingly uses smart machines, with smart people to work with them. It is interesting to note how often, already, organizations talk of their 'intellectual property'. Once again, words signal the way things are going.

The wise organization also knows that their smart people are not to be easily defined as workers or as managers but as individuals, as specialists, as professionals or executives, or as leaders, (the older terms of manager and worker are dropping out of use), and that they and it need also to be obsessed with the pursuit of learning if they are going to keep up with the pace of change.

The wise organization realizes, too, that intelligent individuals can only be governed by consent and not by command, that obedience cannot be demanded and that a collegiate culture of colleagues and a shared understanding is the only way to make things happen. For intelligent, however, do not read intellectual. The words are quite different. 'He may be a great intellectual,' said my daughter of a friend, 'but intelligent he is not. He cannot run a bath, let alone a business, or even his life.'

The pursuit of quality, intelligent machines and intelligent people, a culture of individuals in search of learning and

government by consent – these things hardly seem to add
up to a revolution nor do they describe too many of our
universities and colleges. Yet they are, as we shall see, more
revolutionary concepts than they sound and if they were to
be practised by more organizations then those organizations would be more truly like universities than the
universities themselves.

Quality Is Truth

Quality for instance, has become the new watchword of
many organizations. It is not another gimmick. For too long
too many businesses were concerned with the fast buck, or
the short-term bottom line of residual profit, or, more
technically still, the medium-term earnings per share.
Money was all. With that as your goal it made sense to treat
people as costs to be minimized, to keep tight controls on
everything which might cost money and to reduce as many
operations as you could to a predictable routine. It works
only if nothing ever changes (and so can be rigidly
programmed), if people are unquestioningly obedient (and
so can also be rigidly programmed), and if the cheapest is
regarded as the best.

Four decades ago, inspired by two Americans, Juran and
Deming, the Japanese began to think differently. In the
long-term Deming argued, you stay competitive and in
business by being the best there is, not necessarily the
cheapest, by taking the customer seriously and giving him
or her what they want and need. The product comes before
the money. Quality he maintained, however, is only
achieved if everyone believes in it, if everyone contributes to
it and if everyone is always concerned first of all to improve
their own quality at work. You get quality from quality
people trusted to work positively for the good of the whole
community. Eliminate mass inspection, said Deming, in

what came to be his famous 'fourteen points', drive out fear, break down barriers, get rid of slogans and targets, encourage people to educate and develop themselves to work in teams, to think for themselves, and to believe that everything can be improved forever.

In a more competitive world organizations will only survive if they can guarantee quality in their goods or their services. Short-term profit at the expense of quality will lead to short-term lives. In that sense quality is, to my mind, the organizational equivalent of truth. Quality like truth will count, in the end. No one, and no organization, can live a lie for long. Hard to define, impossible to legislate for, quality like truth is an attitude of mind. It is an attitude which is now at last beginning to infect our organizations. Profit is increasingly recognized as what it always should have been, a means and not an end in itself. It is ironic that it is only now that Deming, in his eighties, has become the Western World's favourite guru, forty years after he started talking this sort of language to the Japanese, who listened and changed.

Quality, however, does not come easily. It needs the right equipment, the right people and the right environment. The effective organization, today, is learning fast to come to terms with the new machines, the new people it needs and with the new culture of consent. It is a new kind of organization in style and temperament, not an easy one to manage or to lead but one which will be increasingly necessary in the competitive knowledge-based world of the future. I call it the Triple I organization only to underline its difference from the organizations we used to know and, very occasionally, to love, but organizations in which most people were not paid to think but to do. In the Triple I organization everyone is paid to think *and* to do, including the machines. It makes a difference, a huge difference, to the way you run the place.

The Intelligent Machines

It is the age of the smart machine. Computers have revolutionized the work of organizations and will go on doing so. One person and a robot can weld a car. No person and a robot can paint it. I went around a sugar refinery worked, in rather unpleasant conditions, in Belgium, by 270 people. One year later I went again. This time it was run by shifts of five people in a carpeted control room with maintenance teams on call.

These things we know are happening. We take others in our stride; the airline can store away our reservations and our dietary requirements and produce them at the touch of a key, it can let us know, instantly, the possibility of any variations to our travel plans and their cost at the touch of a few other keys; we know that the check-out decks at the supermarket already automatically adjust the stock levels and will soon debit our bank accounts; we expect the telephone directory in every country to be computerized and the personnel records of major companies to be accessible via keyboards; we happily pull our cash out of holes in the wall; we know that sophisticated executives can review their spreadsheets on their desk-top terminals; we read of robots re-stacking the shelves in Japanese super-markets; we ride, perhaps, in driverless trains at airports or in Lille in Northern France (and soon, everywhere?); we hear of fifth generation computers which can think for themselves (in a way), and of sixth generation ones with living cells. Technology, as such, holds few fears for most people. It is all, or it should be, in pursuit of better quality.

Smart machines, however, need smart people to work with them, or, sometimes, very dumb people. This book was written at the time when an American warship made a tragic error and shot down an Iranian passenger airline in the Gulf thinking it to be a fighter on the attack. The enquiry made it clear that the computers tracking the plane had made no mistake, but that the relatively young specialists watching the screens in the heat of a battle had misinterpreted the computers' cues. Perhaps, some said then, the smart computer should be allowed to make its own fire or not fire decisions; it might make them better on its own.

Shoshana Zuboff in her book *In the Age of the Smart Machine* describes the conversation in a large pulp mill in North America after a computer-controlled production system had been introduced: 'In fifteen years' time,' the workers said, 'there will be nothing for the workers to do. The technology will be so good it will operate itself. You will just sit there behind a desk running two or three areas of the mill yourself and get bored.'

In fact, as she goes on to demonstrate, it did not turn out like that. Once the workers got used, and it took some time, to running the mill by remote control, by reading the screens rather than by feeling the pipes and squashing the pulp, every small deviation from the norm became a mini-puzzle. The operators would gather round and test out options and possibilities until they found the cause and could put it right. As one operator said, 'Things occur to me now that would never have occurred to me before. With all this information in front of me, I begin to think about how to do the job better. And, being freed from all that manual activity, you really have time to look at things, to think about them, and to anticipate.' Or, as the plant managers said, 'We are depending on the technology to educate our people in abstract thinking ... you can no longer make a decision just based on local data ... you have to derive your decision from the inter-relationships among the variables'; you have to start thinking.

On the other hand, I have stood and watched a man watching a machine count out pills and put them in bottles – watching just in case the machine went bonkers, in which case he pressed a red button, stopped it and called for help.

Or, as one of the pulp workers said, 'Sometimes ... I realize that we stare at the screen even when it has gone down. You get in the habit and you just keep staring even if there is nothing there.'

Smart machines can reduce humans to attendant watch-dogs, but smart organizations see the computers and their machines as aides to clever people. To quote one of Shoshana Zuboff's managers again, 'We never used to expect them to understand how the plant works, just to operate it. But now if they don't know the theory behind how the plant works, how can we expect them to understand all of the variables in the new computer system and how these variables interact?'

Zuboff likes to distinguish between *automating* and *informating*. Automating tends to concentrate on the smart machine and to cut out or reduce people. Informating organizations also use smart machines but in interaction with smart people. In the short-term automating pays off, but informating wins in the longer term because the organization's thinking or 'intellective' capacity has been increased. In this vision the organization is full of colleagues and co-learners, its thinking skill becomes its most precious resource and the challenge of keeping that skill upgraded the major task of the organization. It really has to be a sort of corporate university.

The hard facts of economic life mean that organizations will:

— Increasingly have to invest in smart machines if they want to be as effective as they used to be.
— Increasingly want to use skilled and thinking people to use those machines in order to get the most out of them.
— Need to pay those people more and therefore, if they can, to have fewer of them.

It all puts pressure on the core, a pressure which could be

summed up by the new equation of half the people, paid twice as much, working three times as effectively, an equation which, once you start believing it, has a built-in momentum. To get that three times improvement the smart organization will equip their people with all the technological aids they need, be it car telephones or computers in their homes or audio-printers which translate the spoken word into typescript on the screen, or expert systems which do the first analysis. It will also expect those people to be smart, to be dedicated to their work (none of the leisure age here), and to be prepared to invest enough time and energy to keep ahead of the game, to go on learning, in other words, in order that they can go on thinking.

The Intelligent People

The new organizations need new people to run them, people with new skills, new capacities and different career patterns. More of them, interestingly, are likely to be women, not from any sudden enthusiasm for equality between the sexes, but because organizations will increasingly find that there will not be enough of the skills and the capacities they need if they exclude from their recruitment half of the population.

I was being shown round one of Japan's new businesses – a women's fashion house, designing, making and marketing women's fashions worldwide, although, as it turned out, the actual making was now done in Taiwan (Japan, too, is susceptible to the price of labour). I noticed on my tour that there was an unusually high percentage of women in the offices and, particularly, in the design rooms; nor were they wearing the kind of air hostess uniforms which women in Japanese offices customarily wear. 'Are they allowed to work in jeans and tee-shirts?' I asked. My guide shook his head, scornfully almost. 'They should not,' he said, 'it is not customary, but they are our designers, we need their talent, we have to let them dress as they please.' As in Japan, that bastion of the male executive, so it will be elsewhere.

In Britain it is estimated that 800,000 additional women will join organizations in the next eight years – almost equivalent to the total net increase in the working population. Women, in other words, are poised to take up any extra jobs that are going, plus some that were not going. These will not all be the part-time counter assistants in the supermarkets. Many of them will be the well-educated, qualified women re-entering the workforce.

Organizations will be squeezed, as we have seen, by the need for all the intelligent, qualified people they can get and by the shortage of well-educated, well-qualified youngsters. They will be forced to look to less convenient sources of intelligent people. Some have suggested that the intellectual élite of Africa and China and India will be lured to the West. More obviously, however, organizations will turn first to the pool of talent on their doorstep, the married women with young families.

These women, however, as even the Japanese discovered, will not be men in skirts. They will want proper recognition of their need to raise a family while they are working. Crèches at the office are not the whole answer, although they will be a standard facility by the end of the century. A more flexible way of working is required, one which allows the woman to be at home when she has to be at home, which accepts that full-time attendance in an office is not essential for all types of work, which allows people to work in their own ways as long as the work is done on time and to standard.

The shamrock organization and the federal organization, telecommuting and work centres, are made-to-measure for the working mother. The necessity for organizations to woo more working mothers into their cores will only increase the pressures to move towards these sorts of organizations. In time, then, it will be working fathers as well as working mothers who will be living these more flexible working lives.

In my British paper today there is a picture of the Chalk family, a youngish couple with three small children. The father works from home in the country designing books and educational kits. 'There is no need, today,' he says, 'to work in cities. I like the space and the freedom of the countryside.' His wife, now that the children are starting to go to school, would like to return to the nursing she did when first she was married. Unfortunately, she says, the hours they demand do not permit it. 'Hospitals,' she says, 'have to offer me more flexible work so that I can choose the hours I work to fit in with my family.' They will, Mrs Chalk, they will – because they will have to if they want people with your skills.

The most important difference, however, in the Triple I organizations is the growing realization that everyone in the core will have to be a manager while at the same time no one can afford to be *only* a manager. Smaller numbers in the core require more flexibility and more responsibility. Everyone will increasingly be expected not only to be good at something, to have their own professional or technical expertise, but will also very rapidly acquire responsibility for money, people or projects, or all three, a managerial task, in other words. The days of British India thinking are over, the kind of thinking which boasted in the fact that 2,500 Britons ran India, with the help of technicians, foremen and workers. It was the kind of thinking that led to 'management cadres', management trainees and 'fast-tracks' to the top, for a selected few. I was once one such management trainee, and management was the only role ever expected of me; others would be the experts and the supervisors. It was a business equivalent of British India and the officer class. In future, *everyone* in the core will be an officer and will be expected to be both competent and in command.

In the newer, more hi-tech, organizations in the USA the word 'manager' has begun to disappear. People are not 'managers', they are 'team leaders', 'project heads', 'co-ordinators' or, more generally, 'executives'. They attend *executive* development programmes even though the topic is still that of management. The language is significant, once again signalling a change of attitude and a new way of looking at the world. Managers, after all, imply someone to be managed, they suggest a stratified society. An organization could not logically be staffed only by managers, but it could by executives.

The implications of this shift in thinking are considerable. Management ceases to be a definition of a status, of a class within an organization, but an *activity*, an activity which can be defined, and its skills taught, learnt and developed. The re-definition gives management a professional basis, something which, in Britain at least, it has never had. Management, after all, was held by the British to be akin to parenting, a role of great importance for which no training, preparation or qualification was required; the implication being that experience is the only possible teacher and character the only possible qualification. To study management, when it was seen as a definition of a status, was somehow to suggest that one was unworthy of that status, while 'to manage' as an activity remained a word with a very lowly pedigree in English, meaning colloquially to cope or to contrive, as when one says to one's friend 'did you manage all right today' or 'did you manage to get it working'.

The new respectability

In 1987 two reports castigated Britain's preparation and development of her managers in comparison with other leading industrial nations. The hangover of management as a class was still there. Some of the discrepancies were telling:

— In Japan and the USA some 85 per cent of top managers had degrees whilst the only available comparative figure in Britain was 24 per cent.

— Britain graduated only 1,200 MBAs in 1987 compared with 70,000 in the USA.

— Nearly half of America's 300 biggest companies provided five days off the job training each year for their managers. The comparable figure in Britain (with some noticeable exceptions) was closer to one.

Most would be managers in West Germany do not join their firm until the age of 27 after periods in an apprenticeship, in military service and in 6-year university degrees, whereas the well-educated Britisher joins at 22.

The two reports only confirmed what was long suspected, that British managers were amateurs, sometimes talented amateurs, by comparison with other managers in other countries. The new organizations needed something better.

The reports found ready listeners both among leaders of business and among the young. There was an explosion of interest in MBA degrees, a rush by organizations to link their development plans to some form of qualification and a general readiness to accept that at least the technical knowledge and skills of management, 'business education' as the reports termed it, could be taught and should be taught at an early age even if the human and conceptual skills needed to be honed by experience. The new activity was an outward and visible sign that management was increasingly seen to be the name for an activity and not a class of people. Another discontinuity had occurred even if not everyone perceived it this way at first.

It cannot stop, however, with business education and early qualifications. If executives in every part of the organization, any organization, are to be truly professional they must continue to build on that early base of understanding. Life for a manager, say the Japanese, should be a continual process of self-enlightenment, which is their way of saying that study and learning should never stop. In Japanese organizations, in fact, the seniors spend *more* time on thinking and study than their juniors, reading books and articles; meeting with experts; going on study tours to find out how their competitors work; sitting with their subordinates, *listening* to them not talking at them.

The Japanese are more conscious than most that the other two skills of management, as defined long ago by Professor Katz of Harvard, the human skills and the conceptual skills, are as important as the technical skills. Neither of these two skills can be taught in the classroom, although they can be discussed and debated there; both skills need to be developed by practice, improved by comment, sketched by example; they have to be worked at, for they do not come easily to most people or without effort.

The point about the new organizations is that everyone in the core will increasingly be expected to have not only the expertise appropriate to his or her particular role but will also be required to know and understand business, to have the technical skills of analysis *and* the human skills *and* the conceptual skills and to keep them up to date. Intelligence, for the manager, has three dimensions. The Japanese use mentors to make sure it happens, at least at the beginning. The Americans rely on a philosophy of individual initiative and corporate support which suits their more individualistic culture. The properly intelligent manager, they believe, will develop himself or herself. The British have hitherto relied on a Darwinian belief that the best will come through in the end, but that belief is a wasteful and a cruel philosophy in a world where good jobs are precious and talent rare. The threefold intelligence which the new organizations need in all their people does not just happen. The seeds of intelligence may have to be there in the beginning, at the recruitment stage, but those seeds will need a climate in which to germinate and careful husbandry to let them grow. The intelligent organization has to be a learning organization, at every level.

America's big corporations talk of five days off-the-job training for every executive every year. One British bank is trying to gear up its middle managers to run the kind of federal organization outlined in Chapter 5, and is currently requiring them to spend nine weeks every year on study courses. That is 20 per cent of their working time. Perhaps it should not all be spent on courses, but to expect the intelligent executive to devote one fifth (one day a week) of his or her time preparing themselves for a different and a better future would not be unreasonable in new organizations. It has, after all, long been a tradition of universities that one day a week should be reserved by their faculty for study and research. If all organizations are going to be universities of a sort, pursuing truth in their own fields, running a learning culture, growing new knowledge and new people, then 20 per cent of time devoted to these ends would not be a wasted investment.

The new careers
The new organization will seek to bind its core executives to itself for as long as it thinks it needs them. The new executives, however, will be less ready to be tied, particularly if they have some sort of qualification as a passport. It is rather like the paradox of tenure in universities; those who deserve tenure don't need it and those who need it don't deserve it. In fact, as management becomes more professional, with more professional-type qualifications, the executives will begin to think of their careers as professional careers, as a sequence of jobs which may or may not be in the same organization. Companies, too, will be reluctant to guarantee careers for life to everyone, even in the core. More contracts will be for fixed periods of years, more appointments will be tied to particular roles or jobs with no guarantee of further promotion. The appointments

pages of the papers already reflect this trend: the advertisements offer a job more often than they promise a career.

To the younger new recruit a career is still promised, but the days when the booklet outlining the pension scheme arrives with the letter of appointment are now rare. Whatever they may say, neither the young applicant nor the employer today believe that the appointment is forever. Indeed, fewer and fewer organizations now promise to manage your career; instead they promise opportunities along with help to develop your capabilities to take up some of those opportunities. No longer is there the feeling that somewhere someone is thinking about your future, watching your development, planning your next steps. It probably always was an illusion, now few even pretend. It is a case of 'individual initiative and corporate support', as the Americans describe it.

This change has partly been forced on organizations by the harsher realities of competition. No longer is it possible to carry as passengers those who have failed to live up to their earlier promise or to keep people in jobs which could be done as well by others younger and, usually, cheaper. Partly, however, organizations have found out, too late, that people who have been with the organization for thirty continuous years are not always best able to cope with increasing discontinuity.

I have met too many organizations who have been religiously committed to a policy of growing their own, even recruiting them straight from school at age 15 or 16, only to end up 30 years later with a severe case of group-think at the top, with people who have only known one way of doing things, one set of people, one philosophy; who distrust outsiders, dislike conflict and expect continuity. 'Group-think', as we know from studies of historical events, most famously the 'Bay of Pigs' fiasco early in Kennedy's presidency, comes about when well-meaning people become too close and cohesive to challenge assumptions, to check out facts, to explore new options or to risk too much argument. It is often more important to agree together than to get it right. In conditions of continuity group-think in organizations made for a strong corporate culture, a sense of family, tradition and solidarity. In conditions of discontinuity it leads to falling profits, to merger or takeover, to the end of the cosy club.

Discontinuous change and the new professionalism have therefore combined to spell the end of the corporate career for all but a few. The new executive must look out for himself or herself, remembering that in this new world you are only as good as your current job – the future is not guaranteed. Education in those circumstances becomes an investment, wide experience an asset provided that it is wide and not shallow, and company loyalty something that has to be earned by the company from the individual not demanded of him or her.

Careers will therefore become more variegated. In larger companies there will still be opportunity for variety and advancement, but as these companies get more federal more decisions will be left to the separate parts with the centre left with a brokerage and counselling role. It will increasingly be the individual's responsibility to make sure that the opportunities on offer add up to a sensible career path.

Some will want to interleave their careers with periods of study. We may see an increasing number of formal sabbatical opportunities within universities and business schools to take advantage of this new market. Others, particularly but not only women, will want to interleave the career with periods of raising a family although they might be well-advised to combine this with some form of part-time or distance learning. Some will want intense and early careers allowing them the possibility of a second kind of life before they get too old to do it well. Some will use the organization as a training ground and then, in their thirties, become more independent, perhaps as entrepreneur, perhaps as consultant or professional in the contractual fringe. Most will find that their careers in the organization will in any case begin to peter out in their early or mid fifties when there will still be twenty years at least of active life ahead.

The new executives should be the fortunate ones in the new society. They should have the money and the skills to fill up the 50,000 hours of work beyond the job. They need, however, to prepare themselves for it, to realize that it is going to happen one day, and to them, to look change in the face and see it for what it is – an opportunity as well as a challenge.

One organization has recently dedicated most of its corporate advertising to proclaiming how much time and money it now invests in the education of its executives. It cannot guarantee that it will get a direct return from those who profit from this investment, for some of them will leave for richer pastures and no contract can force them to stay unwillingly, but the quality of its recruits at all levels has increased dramatically. It is a far-sighted response to the new conditions and to the growth of the intelligent organization. It is a response that other organizations need to watch.

The Culture Of Consent

Intelligent people prefer to agree rather than to obey.

In despair at the way its programmes were organized, the Business School in one university recruited as the Director of Programmes a successful businessman, who had made a modest fortune in his own business and wanted to move on to a new career. 'I will soon put some order into this place,' he thought, and said. He wrote memoranda to the academics laying down new procedures. No one read the memoranda. He called a meeting. No one came. In frustration, he asked for an explanation.

'These are independent individuals,' he was told, 'you cannot command them to come to a meeting at your convenience; you have to negotiate a time and place convenient to all of them; you had better send round a list with possible alternatives.' He did and they came, or most of them. He explained the new procedures which, he said, would be introduced next month. At that point one of the older faculty members said, gently,

'Bill, in this kind of institution you cannot *tell* us to do anything, you can only *ask* us and try to persuade us to agree.'

'Well then,' Bill said, 'let me ask you what you think we should do to put some sense into this place.'

'No, Bill,' the elder replied, 'that's what we hired *you* for, to come up with those sort of ideas. But they will only work if we agree with them. If we don't, why then you will have to persuade us or come up with some better ideas. This is, you see, an organization of consent, not of command.'

It is, however, not just because they are intelligent individuals that they cannot be commanded. There is often no one to command them. The new organization, as we have seen, will be a flat organization. Like universities they will often have no more than four layers of executives in any operation. People and groups will have large do'nuts with big areas of discretion. They will be judged increasingly by results not by the methods which they use. Everyone will have their own psychological territory or organizational space, territory which is theirs and which cannot be entered on without permission.

A university lecturer is judged on performance. He or she is in charge of their classroom or seminar. Other colleagues enter only by permission. So it will be with the new organizations.

Nor is it just the flatness of the structures. The new

intelligent machines do not respect herarchical lines of command. They can pass information to whoever needs it, in real time. Intelligent organizations do not ripple their new information systems by pushing the stuff up the ladders and then down again; they encourage the information to go straight to where it is useful. Computers jump organizational barriers and put each group or individual in effective control of their own do'nut.

Mrs Fields' Cookies, in the USA, shows how it is done at its most obvious. Each of the 600 Mrs Fields cookie stores is equipped with a cheap IBM-compatible computer. Linked up with the big computers in the organization's centre in Utah the machines:

(a) plan production. Each shop bakes its own cookies according to a schedule worked out by the computer taking into account past statistics, the weather and how many cookies have been sold in the past hour.

(b) maintain stocks. The computer tells the manager when to re-order.

(c) communicate with top managers. The computer monitors the progress of shop managers towards performance bonuses and runs an electronic mail service.

(d) carry out employee training. The computer drills employees in the knowledge needed for promotion.

(e) organize the accounting and consolidation. The computer keeps track of costs, profits and payroll and analyses them continuously for the local managers.

As a result, with 600 stores, there are only 130 people in headquarters in Park City, Utah, few to command the store managers and not much to tell them that they do not already know.

The Chief Executive of Norsk Data in Norway sums it up, 'Like Japan, we use the consensus method, when the idea is to make the decisions at the appropriate level, which is not always at the top, nor at the bottom, but at the level where the most knowledge is available and where the people are most effective. It means that we must have managers who accept that they cannot force their opinions upon their subordinates. They have to fight like everybody else with their ideas and the best ideas will win, and not necessarily the ones which come from the top or the bottom.

Tom Peters, who co-authored *In Search of Excellence*, described a visit to Johnsville Foods. A typical Johnsville work team, he says:

(a) does its own recruiting, hiring, personnel evaluation and firing;

(b) regularly acquires new skills and then conducts training for everyone;

(c) formulates and tracks its own budgets;

(d) makes capital-investment proposals as needed (with all the necessary staff-work);

(e) is responsible for all quality control, inspection and subsequent trouble-shooting;

(f) suggests and then develops prototypes of possible new products, processes and even business;

(g) works on the improvement of everything, all the time;

(h) develops its own detailed standards for productivity, quality and improvement and makes them tough standards.

This does not, says Peters, leave much for management to do, but then there is not much management, or hierarchy, at Johnsonville.

The point is that you cannot run this sort of organization or these sort of people by command. For one thing the people on the job often have more information than the would-be commander, for another their responsibility for the task is so complete that they are not going to take anyone else's word for something, they need to be convinced. Intelligent organizations have to be run by persuasion and by consent. It is hard work, and frustrating, particularly when the persuasion does not work and the consent is not forthcoming. Bill gave up the Business School in despair and went off to look after a forest, with only the trees to organize.

It is this type of organization which has given rise to what has been called the post-heroic leader. Whereas the heroic manager of the past knew all, could do all and could solve every problem, the post-heroic manager asks how every problem can be solved in a way that develops other people's capacity to handle it. It is not virtuous to do it this way, it is essential. These organizations do not work if it is left to one person. *Everyone* has to be capable or nothing happens. The post-heroic leader lives vicariously, getting kicks out of other people's successes – as old-fashioned teachers have always done.

Let us make no mistake: the cultures of consent are not easy to run, or to work in. Authority in these organizations does not come automatically with the title; it has to be earned. But the authority you need is not based on being able to do the job better yourself but on your ability to help others do the job better, by developing their skills, by liaising with the rest of the organization, by organizing their work more efficiently, by helping them to make the most of their resources, by continual encouragement and example. The job of the leader is a mixture between those of a teacher, a consultant and a trouble-shooter. Technical, human and conceptual skills, the three faces of intelligence, are all required. Some might say it is not a job for normal mortals. It isn't, unless they have grown up with it, have been trained and developed for it, then it can be a most exciting and challenging way to work. As one pulp mill worker said to Shoshana Zuboff, 'If you don't let people grow and develop and make more decisions it's a waste of human life ... Using the technology to its full potential means using the man to his full potential.' That must be good, mustn't it?

Not everyone may think so. It is often easier to be told what to do than to decide for yourself. Choice means responsibility – for failure as well as success. Full potential means full commitment. Some have other things to do. And what, some say, if my full potential is less than is required; what then? The organization of consent puts a premium on competence. There is no place for the incompetent – there are few hiding places in these organizations. Do not look to the new intelligent organizations with their intelligent machines and their cultures of consent for days of gossipy coffee breaks or for boring but untaxing jobs. The culture of consent is not, as the British would say, going to be everyone's cup of tea unless they are educated and prepared for it. There lies the challenge for our society.

Part Three: Living

Introduction

Organizations will never be the same again. That was the message of the first part of this book. It might even have been entitled ' The withering of the corporation' now that it looks as if less than one quarter of the population will have full-time jobs inside any organization.

Does it matter if organizations change or wither? Only to those who work in them, we might think. But here we'd be wrong. When work moves outside the organization, as it is doing, it affects all of us who are on the outside, the great majority. 'What do you do?' no longer means 'What is your job?' but 'How do you occupy your time?' Work has changed its meaning and its pattern. That affects our sense of identity, our families and our roles within those families; our whole way of life is changed, sometimes upside-down.

Will there then be one world and one set of rules for the intelligent and qualified people in the core of the organization and another for those on the edge or on the outside? Even those in the core will be outside for the last third of their lives. When society can no longer assume that we all have a paid job for most of our lives the old recipes for dealing with the small bits at the end (pensions) and the small bits missing (unemployment benefit) become irrelevant. The whole system of money to live on, who gets it and how they get it, needs re-thinking. Discontinuous change requires upside-down thinking by the state.

When education becomes an essential investment, whether as a passport to a core job or as a route to acquiring a saleable skill on the outside, then to ration it is absurd. It is equally absurd to try to shove it all in at the beginning of life, or to think that it can all happen in classrooms, or to ration it later on to those who were cleverest at 18 years of age, or to think that brain skills are the only skills that matter, just because a precious minority need them. A new world of work requires upside-down thinking in education.

Things need to change in the world around us if we are to make the most of the new possibilities, if we are not to keep on trying to use yesterday's answers to deal with the quite different problems of tomorrow. But we also need to change ourselves. A longer life will mean a different life. Success and achievement will have other faces than the ones they wear now. We shall describe ourselves in different ways, live in different ways, have new values and priorities. If we do not, then our children and their children will. Changing has to become a part of our life. We know something about the process of changing, what helps it and what hinders it, how to make it a plus and not a minus, more like learning than losing.

A World To Worry About

If most jobs for the next generation are only going to occupy 50,000 hours (or the equivalent of 25 years) instead of 100,000 hours, there is going to be a lot of space for all of us, sometime, outside the formal jobs, especially since we are all going to live longer. This compression of the job is going to happen, is already happening, *not* because of some miraculous rationing system but because organizations everywhere are learning how to make do with smaller bits of our time. Organizations could once wallow in our time, waste it even, when it was cheap or when everyone around them wasted it as well. A more competitive world and more expensive people demands a more careful use of time. The new technology and new types of organization make it possible to be more careful. Half the people paid double, working twice as hard and producing three times as much, has to be good sense.

Good sense, indeed, but the immediate results could be bizarre, if we are not thoughtful enough in time enough. Half the people working twice as hard while the other half have not enough to do is a worrying prospect. The new rich will not have the time or the energy to enjoy their riches; the leisured class will be those at the bottom of the heap rather than those at the top. An upside-down world.

It is worrying from many points of view. It could be a society obsessed with wealth creation with too little regard to the way that wealth is either spent or distributed. In the end, all societies are remembered more for the way they spend their wealth, than for how they made it. The great civilizations of the past are remembered today for what they did with their wealth, for the monuments they left behind them, for their great buildings, major public works, great art or great conquests, for great education or great social reforms. The pursuit of efficiency and effectiveness in our organizations has got to be a means to something even greater, but if those with the wealth have no time or no thought for its proper spending then we could end up with a society preoccupied only with getting and never with giving or creating.

It could also be a new servant society, with a whole class of people cooking, gardening, driving and maintaining for the busy rich. They might call themselves mini-businesses but their dependency on their new masters is no less because they are now called clients instead of masters. Indeed, because these new servants will be independent and not employees there will be no obligation on the part of the new masters to take any care for their future.

It could become a very divided society; a privileged exclusive world inside the organization for some and a more perilous, exploited and lonely life outside for most; a world in which, if it were dominated by the organization, the educated middle-class professional would have it good and the less-educated would be condemned to be forever the outsider.

Instead of getting more flexible, organizations could react to the shortage of qualified people by becoming *less* flexible, locking in their chosen few with big salaries and bonuses and turning their backs on the freelance or the part-time mother. It would be expensive and, ultimately therefore, dangerous but it would be easier and so may, in the short-term, be more tempting. Such a strategy would only increase the differences between the insiders and the outsiders for a time. The organizations which adapt do best but not all organizations adapt.

It could be a world in which to be old was to be useless because you were not needed by the organization, and old might come to mean over 50. Rich but useless is only marginally better than being poor and useless, particularly if the transition has been from 110 per cent involvement to zero over one weekend.

The divided society could be a mutually envious society, one in which the poor but leisured resent the rich and busy, while the rich and busy resent the drain on their incomes needed to support the new leisured class who have the time they say that they would like to have but not the money.

Maureen Duffy in her book Gor-Saga, a science fiction novel about genetic experimentation, sets the story in a Britain divided between the professional workers, all living in smart urban ghettoes with their own entry controls and pass-cards and working in campus-like offices and laboratories surrounded by high wire fences, and the rest, the 'nons' who, supported by the state, exist in a dreary monotone world of controls and regulations, with no-go areas in the cities and the countryside where guerilla groups hold sway.

I thought it was all fiction until I drove down to dinner one night in the rhododendron belt in Surrey. On turning into the private estate where my hosts lived I found my way barred by a gate. I had to identify myself before I was allowed in. At dinner, later on, discussing possible futures the lady on my right said, 'Of course, the world will inevitably be divided into alphas and gammas and you and I,' she said, politely including me amongst the alphas, 'must be prepared to pay for the gammas to have their fortnight each year on the Costa Brava.' Perhaps, I reflected, driving home, the world of science fiction may not be so fictional after all.

This divided society, this monotone world dedicated to efficiency, this world made for the professional class to dominate, will happen only if we allow the organization to dominate our lives, if all meaning, all status and all money, continue to stem from the 'job', if the 50,000 hours become the only hours that matter, if the first half of this book is the only half which really counts.

Organizations, good organizations, effective organizations, are essential. Jobs, reduced perhaps to 50,000 hours or 25 years, are important to people and to society. The re-shaped organization could, however, enslave us or free us. We shall miss a great opportunity if we do not look beyond the formal organization and beyond the 50,000 hours. Now, for the first time in the human experience, we have a chance to shape our work to suit the way we live instead of our lives to fit our work. We would be mad to miss the chance.

A World That Might Be

Shaping work to suit our lives means, first of all, taking more of the job outside the organization, so that the job is more in our control. That, as we have seen, is already happening. It is still unusual. It is more difficult for the organization to manage the contractual fringe, the independents. It is often a strange experience for the individual. Somehow we have grown used to the fact that organizations should have their own homes. People often like, it seems, to live in two places at once, the office and the family, even if it is not strictly necessary. One small business, exclusively concerned with telephone selling, still insists that the telephone sellers come in to the office to do their telephoning. They happily agree. It is, after all, what everyone does. The cost, however, of all that office space, of the time for coffee and for gossiping, of the inconvenience of the absentees, is making the bosses think again.

The world of work was not always so separate. I grew up in rural Ireland where organizations with their own homes hardly existed other than the local bank and the mill. I hardly knew anyone, as I recall, who went out to work. They lived above the shop they owned, beside the school they taught in, on their farm, above their surgery, next door to their church if they were a priest, or in the same house as their office if a solicitor. Work and life were intertwined. There was one life, not two; one community for each, not two. They were their own men and their own women, not someone else's role occupants. Villages then were places where people lived not just slept at night or relaxed on Sunday.

There will be more like them again. By some estimates one quarter of the working population will be working from home by the end of the century. *From* home is different from *at* home. The home is the base not the prison. We can leave it. There will be organizational work clubs, work centres, meeting rooms and conference centres. We shall not be confined to our terminal in our little back room; there will be people to meet, places to go to, team projects and group assignments. I work from home myself. I go out from it nearly every day, but almost always to a different place. It is not a lonely life.

By taking the job, physically, outside the organization we make it more our own. We have more control over when and how we do it. If we go one step farther and take it contractually outside the organization, becoming in some way self-employed, we make it even more our own. The organization has retreated. It is less dominant, more a helper now than an owner. Jobs do not necessarily belong in organizations any more. It is, when one thinks about it, a significant discontinuity, a change which makes a difference.

It will happen because it will be more economical for the organization. It is therefore, in my view, inevitable. It is up to us to turn the inevitable into an opportunity by seizing the chance to shape our work to suit the way we want to live instead of always living to fit in with our work. It is not always easy. Suddenly we have choice and choice requires decisions. Do you get up now or linger one hour longer in bed? It is a lovely day; should you or should you not take the afternoon off? Do you or do you not labour late into the night to make that piece of work even better still, because there is no one to tell you that it is already good enough? Can one ever dare to take a holiday?

With choice always comes responsibility. The individual gets more freedom but can choose to abuse that freedom by poor quality work, by cheating or by laziness. The organization gets more flexibility but can abuse that flexibility by exploiting the outsider, by tightening its conditions and reducing the rewards. If this world outside the organization is going to be a better world everyone must be conscious of their responsibility as well as of their choices. They may not. That is always the risk in the opportunity and why it is still only a world that might be.

Taking more jobs outside the organization is one part of the opportunity. To take more of our life outside the organization is the other part. It is going to happen, whether we wish it to or not because we are, as I have demonstrated, in the process of splitting the lifetime job in half. Where our fathers thought it normal to spend 100,000 hours, or nearly 50 years, in their organization our children will spend only half of that, whether they cram it into 25 years or spread it out more thinly.

We are taking away 50,000 hours of the job. What will happen in those hours? That is our challenge, and our opportunity. To spend them lying on the beach or sitting in front of endless television serials is one option. Few will take it, partly because they will not be able to afford it, mainly because they will not want it. Endless, mindless leisure has other names – unemployment or imprisonment. Leisure as recreation only makes sense when it is the other side of work, when it is re-creation for more work. Work I am sure, is what we will want to do, work re-discovered, work re-defined to mean more than selling your time to someone else, work that is more in tune with the rest of life, work that is more personal, more creative, more fun than most jobs can ever be.

Those unused 50,000 hours can be our opportunity to discover the missing bits of ourselves, to explore new talents, to add variety to ordinary weeks, to meet new people and to learn new skills. Those unusual hours can add up to a huge new resource for society rather than a pile of unwanted people *if* we start thinking positively, if we find a way to pay for it all, and if, first of all, we start redefining 'work' so that it no longer means only a job. It is not the devil who finds work for idle hands to do, it is our own human instincts which make us want to contribute to our world, to be useful and to matter in some way to other people; to have a reason to get up in the morning.

Put that way, work is the purpose of life, it also gives us a pattern or structure for our days and a chance to meet new people. Purpose, pattern and people, the three Ps at the heart of life. It is odd, then, and sad too, that work has had such a bad press in recent times so that people can even talk of a world without work as some sort of paradise.

It happened, that bad press, because work came to mean only the 'job', and too many jobs were full of toil for others with little sense of mattering, and not much obvious purpose even if the organization, intricate as it is, becomes our great opportunity to put work back into the heart of life. It needs a bit of upside-down thinking to re-invent work, to make it, perhaps, the best of the four-letter words.

7 Portfolios

The Work Portfolio

To re-invent work in its fullest sense we need another word. 'Portfolio' might be that word. It is not, of course, a new word. There are artists' portfolios, architects' portfolios, share portfolios. A portfolio is a collection of different items, but a collection which has a theme to it. The whole is greater than the parts. A share portfolio has balance to it, mixing risk and security, income and long-term gain in proper proportions, an artist's portfolio shows how one talent has more than one way of displaying itself.

A work portfolio is a way of describing how the different bits of work in our life fit together to form a balanced whole. 'Flat people' as E.M. Forster called them, were those who had only one dimension to their lives. He preferred rounded people. I would now call them portfolio people, the sort of people who, when you ask them what they do, reply, 'It will take a while to tell you it all, which bit would you like?' Sooner or later, thanks to the re-shaping of the organization we shall all be portfolio people. It is good news.

The categories of the portfolio
There are five main categories of work for the portfolio: **wage work** and **fee work**, which are both forms of **paid work; homework, gift work** and **study work**, which are all **free work**.

The definitions and the differences are obvious but important – the most important being the difference between paid work and free work. It is free work which has been the missing part of the portfolio in recent times.

Wage (or salary) work represents money paid for time given. **Fee work** is money paid for results delivered. Employees do wage work; professionals, craftspeople and freelancers do fee work. Fee work is increasing as jobs move outside the organization. Even some insiders now get fees (bonuses) as well as wages.

Homework includes that whole catalogue of tasks that go on in the home, from cooking and cleaning, to children and caring, from carpentry to shopping. Done willingly or grudgingly, it is all work.

Gift work is work done for free outside the home, for charities and local groups, for neighbours or for the community.

Study work done seriously and not frivolously is, to me, a form of work not recreation. Training for a sport or a skill is study work, so is the learning of a new language or a new culture, so are the long days I spend reading other peoples' books in preparation for writing my own.

In the past, for most of us, our work portfolio has had only one item in it, at least for men. It was their job or, more grandiosely, their career. This was, when you think about it, a risky strategy. Few would these days put all their money into one asset, yet that is what a lot of us have been doing with our lives. That one asset, that one job, has had to work overtime for we have looked to it for so many things at once – for interest or satisfaction in the work itself, for interesting people and good company, for security and money, for the chance of development and reality. The list of things which people say that they want from their jobs has been consistent over the years; the problem has always been that we looked for the whole list from one job – no wonder, in retrospect, that so many have been disappointed.

For some, for those in the core of the shamrock, things will not change noticeably. Indeed, because work in the core will be more pressured, more consuming and more involving, the job will fill the whole portfolio to bursting point with just one item. There will be room for nothing more, even at times for family and fun as long as they remain in that core.

The message of the 50,000 hours, however, is clear. These busy busy jobs in the core will not last for ever or for as long as they used to, or even for as long as their occupants would like them to. It will be called age discrimination, no doubt, but we shall come to realize that high energy jobs in the knowledge-based organizations of the future do require younger people. Swimmers fade in their late teens, tennis players in their late twenties, chess-players in their thirties, journalists in their forties, and who knows what happens to money-dealers after thirty? We shall become used to the idea that the full-time executive or skilled worker fades in his or her late forties, in most occupations, and, if you believe any of the earlier chapters, *everyone* in the role will be either an executive or a skilled worker.

There will be glorious exceptions, and there will be some who will fade into different glories, becoming coaches or mentors or managers to the newer stars, swapping energy for wisdom. But wisdom is a part-time role. As his partner said to my friend, 'We value your wisdom greatly, John, and would love to have you around, but only on Tuesdays.' Nor is it always the best tennis players who become the best coaches. It is happening already today in those organizations whose *only* assets are their talented people – in advertising, in consultancy, in design – the energy roles are increasingly going to people in their thirties and forties, with the wisdom roles 'confined to Tuesdays'.

For the core people, the full portfolio of work only begins to expand after the job ends. The most difficult transition for them is in fact from a one-item portfolio to a multi-item one, not to an empty one. The transition is always a very personal bit of discontinuous change and one to which people could with advantage apply a bit of upside-down thinking. Alas, however, too many of the core seek to perpetuate the only concept of work which they have known, the full-time job in an organization, wage work at its best.

William came to see me one day. He was 48 and a senior account director and board member of a big advertising agency. The Chairman had just told him that they felt he should 'move on', leave them at the end of the year, along with one year's extra salary, the gift of his car and so on. It was a generous leaving present.

'I need another job,' said William. 'Have you any ideas?'

'What are you good at?' I asked him.

'I don't know, really. Running an account group in advertising, I suppose.'

'Why don't you try this,' I said. 'Ask twenty people who know you well, at work or outside work, to tell you just *one* thing which they think you do well. That's all. Not a critique of your personality just one thing you do well, in their experience of you.'

'O.K. I'll try it,' he said.

He found it difficult. He was a reticent Englishman, after all. But he came back in a fortnight looking puzzled but happy. 'I've got a list of twenty things,' he said. 'Quite surprising, some of them. Funny thing, though,' he added, 'none of them mentioned running an account group.'

'Maybe that's why it's time to move on!' I said. He didn't smile. We looked at his list in some detail. We discussed lots of ways, little ways, in which he could put his talents to use. There were ideas there for little business ventures, for voluntary activities, for some teaching, for personal learning, for some writing. None of them, however, added up on their own to a full-time proper job. He still did not smile.

He went back to advertising in the end, not as an account director, but as director in charge of administration in another and smaller agency. It was a proper job, but in a couple of years' time he will be around again, I suspect. Perhaps by then he will be able to accept that one full-time job in advertising is not the only nor even the best way to deploy his many and considerable talents. We are all, however, the children of our times, or, more accurately, the children of yesterday's times. Discontinuity in careers was not part of those times, nor were portfolios of different sorts of work.

For those now in the core, however, such discontinuity looks increasingly likely in their mid-fifties. For their children it will more likely be in their early fifties if not before. Nor are there going to be many alternative core jobs available. Like it or not, the ex-core employee will be forced into a portfolio life, and life without *some* work, as any of the long-term unemployed will confirm, is life without meaning. Portfolios stuffed only with memories soon gather dust.

Already the fashion is changing. 'Early retirement' used to be words spoken in a hush. The end of the job meant the end of life to many. Now you will hear many a person boast of how they have 'managed to arrange early retirement'. It has become a technical term signifying release or a key to new possibilities. Ask those people what they will do next and they do not talk of wage work but of ways of keeping their hand in (some small free work), of time for old enthusiasms, or new causes and hobbies (gift work), of helping out more with household chores or parenting (homework) or of taking up a new interest (study work). They don't call it work, but they should. They are building up a new portfolio and in so doing re-defining their lives and themselves. Early retirement is not the right word for them.

For others, the portfolios will have a different balance. It is not everybody's wish to work 45 hours a week or even more for someone else – although a Government minister spoke recently of her 100 hour-a-week job – and, statistically, half of all those in paid work won't be able to anyway.

For them the portfolio will be more varied. Sometimes there will be two or more part-time jobs (nearly 1 million Britons officially declare two jobs), sometimes they will save money rather than make money by increasing their self-sufficiency at home. Homework can often be a form of self-paid fee work. For many, small bits of proper fee work, or part-time self-employment, becomes an integral part of their way of life. They think of it as 'extra', money for the kids' presents, or for holidays – pocket-money. The authorities call it moonlighting and illegal. It is both, of course; understandable *and* illegal.

For many women, paid work has to give way to free work when they start to raise a family. As any woman will tell you a family is work, however much you love them. Understandably, many women want proper recognition for it, money to put it bluntly, but that is to play along with the conceit that only paid work counts. As more men re-balance their portfolios it should be increasingly possible for more women to put serious bits of paid work into their portfolios. Indeed, as I have argued earlier, organizations will increasingly need them and their skills, while the new technology and the new kinds of organizations will make it all much easier for them to fit bits of fee work into their lives.

Portfolios of work are not new. Small businesses have portfolios of products or of clients. Large businesses have portfolios of smaller businesses. As more and more people move their paid work outside organizations, or are moved, they are pushed or lured into becoming small independent businesses. They are paid in fees, not wages, and have to develop their own portfolios of customers and of activities.

From portfolios of customers, or products, it is an easy step to move to seeing some customers as free, some products or activities as non-financial, to include free work in the plans for the week or for the year. The free worker is by temperament a portfolio worker as is the working mother who has always had to juggle the demands of her time, and who knows that the responsibilities are no less just because the money is less. Free work is as serious as paid work.

Professionals, who charge fees, know about portfolios. So do craftsmen, particularly those who work for themselves by themselves. The plumber, the electrician, the weaver and the potter have to juggle the demands on their time like any mother. Too many customers leaves no room for anything else, even for the paperwork. Too few customers, of course, leaves no money for the bread.

Portfolios accumulate by chance. They should accumulate by choice. We can manage our time. We can say no. We can give less priority, or more, to homework or to paid work. Money is essential but more money is not always essential. Enough can be enough. Without deliberate choice portfolios can become too full. The irony of modern life is how busy people can be in what is meant to be a time for more leisure.

It is no bad discipline to calculate the days (or hours) spent each year (or week) on the different parts of the portfolios. My own portfolio, as a professional man in his Third Age, is as follows: 150 days fee work (at varying rates and including provision for administration, paperwork and abortive meetings with clients); 50 days gift work (for various associations, societies and groups); 75 days study (essential to keep up-to-date in my work); 90 days homework and leisure (it is hard to distinguish between the two).

Ninety days of domestic work and leisure looks a lot. It is salutary to remember that most people take 137 days (52 weekends plus 5 weeks holiday plus 8 public holidays). The danger of a portfolio life can, ironically, be that there is too much work since there is no one to say 'this is not a working day'.

Where will the money come from?
That is always the central issue in planning a portfolio. The

answer, once again, is from a portfolio of things. Portfolio people think portfolio money not salary money. They learn that money comes in fits and starts from different sources. There may be a bit of a pension, some part-time work, some fees to charge or things to sell. They lead cash-flow lives not salary lives, planning always to have enough in-flows to cover out-flows when both can be, to some extent, varied. Invoices sent and paid promptly with bills paid late has helped to keep many a small business financed, and portfolio people too.

'What sort of money do you earn?' I asked my friend Percy as we motored in his Jaguar from his shipbroking office to his house in the country. I was genuinely curious to know what it needed to live in his style.

'I've no idea,' he said.

'Come on,' I said. 'To the nearest two thousand, you must know.'

'Honestly, I don't,' he protested, and then, as I looked disbelieving, he asked, 'Look here, how much sugar do you use in your house in a year?'

'I've no idea.'

'Of course not, but I bet there's always sugar there. So it is with money, I don't add up the totals but I make sure there's enough coming in to pay the bills when they come in. If Paul McCartney can go out to work to earn a swimming pool I can do something when I have to pay the parking fines.'

It sounded very grand but I gradually discovered that that is how all small businessmen quite properly think, although it is not always that easy to find that something to do to pay the extra bills when we need to.

Portfolio money is a way of thinking. Portfolio people think in terms of barter. They exchange houses for holidays, babysit for each other, lend garden tools in return for produce, give free lodging in return for secretarial help in the evenings. Portfolio people know that most skills are saleable, if you want to sell them. If you love designing houses, design someone else's; if you like photographing dogs, photograph other people's dogs; if you like driving, drive other people's errands – and charge a fee if you need money. The fee can be as small, or as big, as you think fit; small for the first-time seller, big if you feel confident or if you do not really care whether you do it or you don't. Hobbies can be mini-businesses for portfolio people, their cooking can be their skill, their plants their merchandise.

Saleable skills and mini-businesses are the where-withals of portfolio people. If they do not have them they need to acquire them, preferably before they start. This is the almost legal informal economy, only illegal when not declared to the tax man. It is growing rapidly, probably accounting for quite a lot of the gap in every country's national accounts, the gap between what they know we spend and what we say we earned. In the USA that gap is nearly $10 billion of missing money. We are seeing the consequence of taking work outside the organization, of taking work outside the formal job.

Portfolio Marriages

Everyone will live a portfolio life one day for part of their lives. Most people will match that with a portfolio marriage. A portfolio marriage is not a recipe for polygamy, a different partner for each day or night, nor is it an invitation to serial monogamy, a sequence of husbands or wives. Rather it is a way of adjusting a marriage to the differing demands of a changing portfolio in life.

Marriages have always needed to adjust to the stages of life, through child-rearing, to adolescence, to the empty nest and retirement. The new requirements of the workplace, the move towards more portfolio lives, more paid work for qualified women, more work from home and more telecommuting, the increase in earlier retirement, second careers and Third Age re-thinks, these all have their impact on the marriage. If the relationship does not flex in some way it will break. Too often, serial monogamy or a change in partner is the way many people match their need for a marriage with the need for change.

Portfolio thinking is one way of changing the marriage without changing the partners. It becomes increasingly important as an accompaniment to portfolio work lives. The idea originated in a piece of research which I did some years ago with Pam Berger at the London Business School. The research set out to explore how some successful managers in mid-career combined their busy executive lives with their family lives.

Some background is essential. The managers, all male in those days, had all been participants in a long executive development programme at the London Business School. They were in their mid-thirties with good jobs in large organizations. Twenty-three of them agreed to participate in the study. It was therefore a rather special sample, small, successful, well-educated and happily married (or they would not have agreed to participate). We cannot therefore say that everything which this group of people told us applies to all couples or even to all executive couples, nevertheless the marriage patterns which emerged do seem to make sense to a lot of people to whom I subsequently presented the study.

I knew all the men personally. Pam Berger did not. She therefore did all the interviews and the questionnaires, arranging always to meet the man first at his office, to travel home with him, to meet his wife and children, to meet with the wife alone and then with them both together. They filled in some standard questionnaires, responded to interview schedules and generally talked about the pressures on their lives and how they responded to them. We were looking for practical clues to managing marriages and work. We found none that were common to all. Instead we found a set of marriage patterns.

In their responses to one questionnaire (the Edwards Personal Preference Schedule) which draws out an individual's priorities and preferences, this group and their wives had unusually extreme scores on four dimensions: Achievement (ACH) or the need to succeed in something; and Dominance (DOM) or the need to have power and influence, which were highly correlated with each other; and Succourance (SUC) or the desire to help and support, which was highly correlated with nurturance (NUR), the work to take care of someone. Both of these, interestingly, corresponded closely with low scores on Autonomy (AUT), the desire to do your own thing. We were therefore able to put these scores together on a chart (see below) and to put an X for the position of each of the forty-six individuals in the twenty-three marriages.

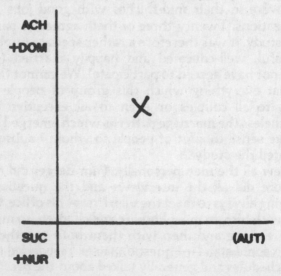

We then divided the chart into four quarters and gave them letters.

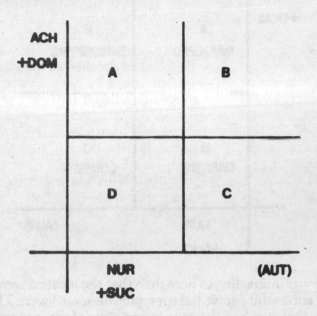

To make it more interesting we gave names to the four quarters. B was the archetypal western man, achieving, dominant, autonomous with little interest in helping or caring. We called this box the **Thrusters**. A, by contrast, was achieving and dominant but was at the same time interested in helping and caring for people, scoring low on autonomy. We called the A box the **Involved**. C we called the **Loners**, for they scored low on everything except Autonomy, and D we called the **Carers** because that was what they scored highly on, being uninterested in Achievement or Dominance.

The box now looked like this:

It was interesting to note then that the most conventionally successful people (salaries, job titles, etc.) were Thrusters, that over half the women and none of the men were in
box D, Carers, that the Industrial Chaplain and the Civil
Servants were in box A, the Involved, and that only one of
the women, a full-time working wife was in Box B, a
Thruster.

The distribution of the sexes would not be the same
today, when at least a quarter of the executives on that
programme are now women. This was, after all, in 1974.
The world has changed, but probably not the marriage
patterns which then emerged from this analysis.

With forty-six individual crosses on our chart, the
marriage patterns emerged when we joined the crosses up
to see which was married to which. There are sixteen

different possible combinations of the four boxes, but only four of those combinations were relevant to this group. They were:

— The B-D marriage, a Thrusting man married to a Caring woman (this was by far the most common of the patterns).
— The A-A marriage, of two 'Involved' people, (the second most common pattern).
— The C-C marriage, of two Loners (there were two of those).
— The B-B marriage of two Thrusters (of which there was only one in this sample, but probably more common today).

Each of these patterns was quite different, reflecting the different combinations of the partners' preoccupations at that stage in their lives, a stage when most of them had been married for five to ten years, had between one and three children and a home of their own.

The patterns start to come alive when the way these couples lived is described. The B-D pattern was a marriage in which the roles of everyone and everything were clear and separate. It was the husband's job to earn the living, the wife's to run the home and look after the children. He looked after the drink in the house, she the food, he tended the vegetables, she the flowers. He had his friends, she hers. There were no overlapping friends except for family.

Even the rooms had separate roles – there were sitting-rooms and dining-rooms, studies and bedrooms. The children knew their place and their manners and went to bed when told. Conversation at meals was about things or events ('When is your mother coming to stay?' 'What is wrong with the hoover?') rather than ideas. We asked them what they did when they felt under stress. They moved away from each other, he to dig in the garden or hit a golf ball, she to suffer in silence in the bedroom – separate again. Interestingly, they usually came from the same part of the country but he was two or three years older and had three years more education than her (i.e. had been to university whereas she had not).

These seemed to be very secure marriages at the time. Everyone knew their role and everything went according to a schedule. Where his work led she followed, managing the home base for his career.

The A-A marriages were quite different. Here the partners were of the same age and had the same sort of education, in fact in this sample they had usually met at college. In these marriages the roles were overlapping, as were their homes. Both partners worked, although for her it was usually a part-time job. However, both took turns at child-minding and whoever felt hungry did the cooking. The rooms had no clearly defined roles, kitchen, living, dining, study were all one, bedrooms doubled as work-rooms, meals were haphazard and casual, the children precocious, advanced or ill-manne.ed, depending on your viewpoint.

The lives of both partners were intertwined. All friends were joint friends, all activities joint activities. Mealtime conversations were about ideas, were full of argument and discussion. When they had stress problems they shared them, drinking copious cups of coffee or cheap red wine late into the night then going off to be concerned but achieving workers the next day. Life was intense, interesting and, yes, involved.

The B-B marriage was different again. It was a very competitive partnership. There were no children and the wife earned as much as her husband in the same line of business. They were, therefore, a full dual career couple with what might be called, at that time, a low-slung lifestyle, low-slung cars, low-slung furniture, low-slung clothes, all quite expensive because they were the dinkies of their time

(Dual Income No Kids Yet). They argued a lot, discussed business more than ideas, and took their stress out on each other. The competition however was tempered by mutual affection; they were friendly rivals, so much so that she applied to follow her husband on the executive programme in order not to be left behind.

Lastly there were the C-C marriages. These were the partnerships of two people very similar in age and disposition and background who each wanted, above all else, to be able to do their own thing. Neither was hungry for success or for other people. They were very self-sufficient and encouraged the same in their children. In one home it was carried to extremes; there was no communal sitting room, no chairs to sit on except in the individual bedrooms. There was a kitchen but each member of the family got their own food. They lived their own lives, timing things precisely in the case of one couple, so that he would arrive home just in time for her to leave to go out to her work with one of them at home with the children. They were content, they said, and happy – two trees together in the wood, together but not touching, or even talking very much.

One conclusion from all this was just that it takes all sorts to make the world. As we discussed the findings with more people, however, we heard the same comments again and again:

— 'It is a snapshot of relationships at a particular stage. It would be interesting to know how they change over time.'
— 'My marriage started off as an A-A marriage. We shared everything. But the children came, my job hotted up, we moved to the country and, yes, we are now a B-D couple.'
— 'My firm assumes, I think, a B-D marriage because we ask an awful lot from our people and they need a secure base at home with no worries.'
— 'I gave up my career when I had the children – I had to because John was terribly stretched at work and could not

help – but I hope to get back to work and to an A-A pattern one of these days.'
— 'Your chart describes my life, an A-A start, moved to B-D when we had the kids, C-C when they left, and last month we divorced – nothing to say to each other any more, each with our own lives to lead now.'
— 'We try to live an A-A life but it has meant turning down two promotions because we would have had to move and I'm not sure that we can continue like this.'
— 'We think we try all the patterns in one year. A lot of the time it is a B-D marriage with one stuck at home with the kids, but at weekends it is definitely A-A because we do everything together while we always have separate holidays in the summer –C-C.'

The chart, I now believe, is a good although crude description of the options open to a relationship. The strong relationship is one that is flexible enough to move from one pattern to another when the need demands. It is a portfolio of possibilities. Most relationships these days start in an A-A mode, a partnership of equals sharing most things. The pressures of a job on one or other of the partners, together with children, lead to a B-D relationship – for a time. In our sample even the competitive B-B marriage moved to B-D when the children arrived, apparently to the satisfaction of the wife.

Not many women, however, are content today with the D or caring role for too long. They have tasted the excitement of paid work, domesticity is dull and lonely, they would like to mingle some fee work or study work with homework. Ideally, they would like to work back to A-A but this requires the husband to give up some of his priorities for autonomy and independence and move from B to A at the same time.

If a return to A-A is impossible then B-B is an option, the full dual career. It requires a lot of energy, organization and money to keep two successful careers going and a home. It can easily slip down to C-C with thoughts of achievement and power abandoned in favour of continued independence. It is hard, it seems, to go anywhere from a C-C position except out of the chart altogether.

More interesting, still, is the possibility in a dual portfolio life of mixing the patterns monthly, or weekly, or even daily. A truly flexible relationship can have B–D days, A-A weekends, C-C holidays and D-B spells (with the man doing the home-making and the caring), or some other combination.

The research made it clear that there is no optimal pattern for a marriage. All patterns are possible. It seems essential to have a joint understanding of what the pattern is, how and when it might change, what the consequences are of living in a certain pattern and what are the costs and benefits. People clearly *can* change their pattern if both parties want to. Separation and divorce often seem to occur because one partner wants to change the pattern and the other does not.

Bill and Frances had been married 26 years. Their children had all by now left home. Bill was 53 and at the height of his career as a marketing executive in a multinational company. Frances had minded the home and supported his career, moving home and country three times. Now she would, she felt, at last have the opportunity to develop her own career, at the age of 49. She enrolled in art college, with Bill's enthusiastic support, she met new friends, developed new skills and new interests. She went on trips with them, not as a spouse to Bill's conferences, she had them home to meals instead of Bill's business associates. They no longer planned their weeks together as they used to do but kept to their own schedules. Both were busy. Their old friends seldom saw them. Suddenly, one Sunday morning, Bill left home. 'I was a stranger there,' he said, 'Frances has gone into another world where I can't follow her. She has left the marriage so I might as well leave the house where I no longer belong and find another home.'

The irony is, of course, that Bill's career job will finish in a year or two. He will need new interests. A C-C pattern might in their case have been a necessary interlude after long years of a B-D pattern before returning to more of the A-A relationship they had when they first met. Two portfolio lives would then need a portfolio marriage, moving between the patterns. If they do not realize, however, that is only the *patterns* which are changing then it is the *relationship* which breaks. Portfolio thinking *and* talking are both essential.

In Praise Of Portfolios

Bits and pieces of work sound a poor second best to a proper job and a proper career. They often are, but they do have great compensations. In 1988 the Henley Forecasting Centre in Britain surveyed the attitudes to work of 2,000 people. They asked them to give a percentage ranking to what they found the most important aspect of their work. The list came out like this:

1. Having control over what to do. 50%.
2. Using knowledge and experience to make decisions. 50%.
3. Having a variety of things to do. 39%.
4. Amount you earn. 35%.
5. Being with and making friends. 21%.
6. Doing a job that you know people respect. 19%.

(The AB socio-economic group put money even lower at 25% and variety higher at 62%.)

A portfolio life sits rather well with those attitudes and

better than most full-time jobs. The things it lacks – a job title to swank about and lots of congenial company – do not seem to be of much interest. Nor is the money. That's all very fine, one might think, for those who have the money and the job title. For those without them a portfolio life will seem distinctly insecure. That is true. A portfolio existence comes easiest in the Third Age when, for many, a house is largely paid for and the children are self-supporting when, perhaps, some savings have accumulated or a part-pension is coming nearer, and when there is at least a job title in the past to reminisce about.

On the other hand, most households now are portfolio homes, with more than one income coming in. Arguably, a tolerable lifestyle is not possible for many households without multiple incomes. Collections of portfolios are themselves a kind of security for not everything goes wrong at once, whereas the one income family is perilously dependent on that one income. Should that one income go, as many studies have shown, there is nothing to fall back on, no other tradition of work or of money-making, no idea of self-sufficiency or of entrepreneuring, no sharing of roles, nothing except an abundance of time and a lack of cash. Employment can be riskier than self-employment, even for the whizz-kids of the money world where they can be fired at ten minutes notice, not allowed even to return to their desks. A high salary or a good wage guarantee neither security nor freedom.

Ray Pahl ends his fine compendium of papers *On Work* with a powerful image of a woman ironing. She might, he points out, be a homeworker for a laundry working in piecework for a miserly rate but as an essential part of the family's income; she might, on the other hand, be making pin money for herself by a spot of occasional extra work; she might be ironing a blouse for her evening out or a shirt for her lover, as a token of her affection; or it might be part of Monday's daily grind; she might even be doing it for a sick neighbour or to prepare a costume for the local dramatic society. Should it not, indeed, be a person ironing rather than a woman? Pahl observes, however, that if he had used the word 'person' most people would still instinctively have interpreted it as 'woman'. Will they still do so in ten years' time, I wonder.

Pahl's point is that it is all work and always will be. It is social attitudes and social constructions of work which change. If ironing for a wage disappears we shall perhaps do more ironing for love. My point would be that there have, indeed, always been all sorts of ironing, some done with a scowl on the face, some with a smile. It is and always has been a portfolio of ironing; but the portfolio can change, as the times change, as our circumstances change, as our relationships change and as our tastes and priorities change. That is good news. All work is becoming like ironing; a portfolio of choice and necessity. That could be even better news. After all, as Noel Coward said, 'Work is much more fun than fun.' It is, but only if it is work of our choice under our control, if we are all Noel Cowards of a sort.

Leisure, if we think about it, is only truly leisure when it is part of a portfolio, not the whole of it. The idea of a 'leisure society' with whole blocks of people with nothing to do except enjoy themselves, is to me a vision of hell not of heaven. The best form of leisure is nearly always active leisure, or work of a sort. The point is that the activity is of our choice, in our time and under our control. When we have had enough of it we can stop.

This chapter has largely been addressed to the career executive of the big organization because it is his or her way of life which will change most radically in an Age of Unreason and because it is they and their families who will find the idea of portfolio lives most strange. The chapter would, however, be no news at all to all those who have always lived their lives outside organizations – small farmers, craftsmen and skilled artisans, such as plumbers and carpenters, small shopkeepers and publicans, lorry drivers and taxi-drivers, artists and furniture restorers, gardeners and plant-hire people. The world of East Anglia, where I live, is full of such people, so are Italy and Southern Ireland where I visit. So is the USA where I was told 'In this country, everyone is first a business person and then something else.' Those people, the independent ones, well understand the necessity of a portfolio life. It may not be as rich or as varied a portfolio as they would like, or as much fun, but they know instinctively that life has to be a mixture, that work does not fit neatly into five days of eight hours, that money comes from many quarters and in different ways, that no one person or organization owns you – and most of them would have it no other way.

8 Re-inventing Education

If changing is really learning, if effective organizations need more and more intelligent people, if careers are shorter and more changeable, above all, if more people need to be more self-sufficient for more of their lives then education has to become the single most important investment that any person can make in their own destiny. It will not, however, be education as most of us have known it, the old-fashioned learning derided in Chapter 3 or the old British notion of education as something to be got rid of as soon as one decently could.

Education needs to be re-invented. Our schools first need to be re-designed for they are not immune to the principles of the shamrock or of federalism. But education will not finish with school, nor should it be confined to those who shine academically at 18. Learning, too, as we have seen, happens all through life unless we block it. Organizations therefore need, consciously, to become learning organizations, places where change is an opportunity, where people grow while they work.

These things will not happen automatically. The changes needed require some upside-down thinking, initiatives by government and determination by organizations. It is no exaggeration to say that we need to re-invent education if we are going to avoid the worst scenarios in this book and to profit from the best.

The Shamrock School

The ideas of the shamrock and federalism could turn schools upside-down. At present schools are bedevilled by the need to offer choice to a wide variety of students without running foul of the bureaucracy and anonymity that is inevitable in a large organization.

I stood one day and watched twenty double-decker buses disgorge hundreds upon hundreds of teenage girls into a cathedral to celebrate a school's silver jubilee. It was the first time that anyone had even seen the whole school gathered together in those twenty-five years. To me, watching, 1,500 girls was an awe-inspiring and a rather intimidating spectacle. Why, I wondered would anyone want a school so big that it could only meet in a cathedral? The answer is simple. Comprehensive education requires comprehensive institutions. If sixteen subjects are to be offered in the top class to a minimum of ten pupils per class, you will need, working backwards 1,400 pupils in an 11–18 age-range school. More choice at the top would mean proportionately more people lower down to provide the numbers needed in each class. Small schools may be nice in theory, they told me then, but they restrict choice.

One answer is to hive off the top, creating specialist colleges for the seventeen and eighteen year olds and leaving smaller schools behind for the younger ones. I suppose that principle could be carried even further with schools for the 11–13, 14–15, 16–18 age groups, but being so specialized in age they would not be very satisfactory communities for teachers to work in, or for students to study in, and they would inevitably cost more.

The alternative is to think upside-down and turn the school into a shamrock with a core activity and everything else contracted out or done part-time by a flexible labour force. The core activity would be primarily one of educational manager, devising an appropriate educational programme for each child and arranging for its delivery. A core curriculum would continue to be taught directly by the school but anything outside the core would be contracted out to independent suppliers, new mini-schools. There might then be a range of independent art schools, language schools, computing schools, design schools and others. These independent suppliers would be paid, by the core school, on a per capita basis, probably with an agreed minimum.

The job of the school proper would be to set and monitor the standards of these mini-school outsiders, to ensure an adequate variety, to help students and their families decide on an educational programme from all that was available and to manage a core curriculum itself in order to maintain some sense of group cohesion at the centre.

In this way the school as a whole could be quite big because for most of the time the students would be in smaller mini-schools. The parents would choose, not so much between schools as within schools, between the variety that was on offer. In big schools there could be a number of competing outside institutions offering courses in one particular area, such as art or languages.

The point, as always with the shamrock, would be flexibility. You do not make your suppliers redundant, you simply do not renew the contract. In a way it happens already. Work experience is now becoming part of the normal curriculum for 14–16 year-olds. Since work experience cannot, by definition, happen anywhere except in real work organizations, this part of the curriculum has, in effect, to be contracted out, although not for a fee.

Schools will say that it will be more difficult to organize. The shamrock always is more difficult; but it does provide more flexibility, too. The school need not now be run totally on an age-graded basis. The student who is gifted at language school could progress faster, irrespective of age, even though the core groups in the school proper would still be year groups. Everybody progresses at different rates in different subject areas – the shamrock design makes it feasible to recognize this. Of course the school day would have to change. The variety could not be programmed into the 35-minute slots beloved of school bureaucrats. The core curriculum could be taught on four mornings a week leaving the fifth day and every afternoon, and evening, for the mini-schools. There is, after all, no reason why every student has to finish school at the same time or could not learn to have a free afternoon followed by an early evening session in his or her design school. It is, come to think of it, more like the world of work they will be entering.

The shamrock federal school could go even further. It could give each student their own inverted do'nut in the form of an individual contract. In this contract there would be a core which the school would undertake to deliver and the individual to study. There would then be an area of discretion, out of which the student could pick a range of options. There would be a clear definition of goals and measures of success for the do'nut as a whole, including the demonstration of capacities, such as interpersonal skills, practical competences and organizing abilities which cannot be fully taught in classroom subjects. There would be planned opportunities to review and, if necessary, to revise the contract, on both sides.

This idea of an individual contract with each student, currently under study in Britain by the National Association of Head Teachers, becomes much more plausible when the school has the flexibility of the shamrock and is really a federation of mini-schools. It would change the relationship between student and school making it more one of partnership under contract and less one of teacher and child or warden and prisoner. School would be seen by more young people as a personal opportunity not a chore, they would be more like customers for some of the time, carrying a per capita income with them to the mini-schools they choose.

Everybody might begin to take themselves and everybody else more seriously.

Some of it is happening already. I telephoned a large community school, where adults study as well as teenagers and where activities go on until late into the evening. I asked to speak to the Head. 'Which Head?' said the receptionist, 'there are several heads of several schools here.' It was the outward sign of a federal shamrock.

Upside-Down Schools

Some years ago I was commissioned to study the organization of some of Britain's schools. I went to visit some typical big city centre comprehensive secondary schools. I remember that my first 'getting to know you' question on those cold November mornings was always 'How many people work here?' I always got the same sort of numbers, between seventy and ninety people. When I mentioned this, in some surprise to a Chief Education Officer, he exclaimed, 'Oh dear, they left out the cleaners.' 'No,' I replied, 'they left out the children.'

This was odd because at an earlier briefing session with the head teachers I had asked them what they saw as the role of the children in their schools, in comparison with other organizations. They are the workers, they said unanimously, while we teachers are the managers and the instructors. The early morning instinctive response was the right one, however, because who would expose workers to an organization which required them to work for ten different bosses in one week, in three or four different work groups, to have no work station or desk of their own but to be always on the move? What sensible organization would forbid its workers to ask their colleagues for help, would expect them to carry all relevant facts in their heads, would require them to work in 35-minute spells and then move to a different site, would work them in groups of thirty or over and prohibit any social interaction except at official break times.

The typical secondary school, I had to conclude, does not really think of its students as workers. Nor are they the customers, for they have no real choice, no consumer power, no right to complain or to be asked for their preference. Schools do not do much market research among their students. Instinctively, I felt, schools see their students as their products.

Organizationally, that made sense. Products start off as raw material. The material is processed, in batches usually, at different work stations. It is graded and inspected, so are students. The fact that some 40 per cent are below par is regarded mainly as a sign that standards are high. Unfortunately, the inferior batch is not sent back for further processing but is turned out to fend for itself in the world of work.

That world of work, however, is quite different. In that world people work on tasks in mixed ability groups. Mixed ability in the world of work means a group of people with different abilities of the same level. In schools mixed ability means people with the same ability but different levels. In schools collaborating is cheating, in work it is essential. In work 75 per cent quality is not good enough, in schools it is excellent. In work people see the result of their labours weekly, sometimes even hourly – success and achievement are obvious, and most people feel some success and some achievement each week. In schools success is rationed and you have to wait the best part of a term for it in many places. At work, your output is useful to someone somewhere, at school it is only useful to yourself. Work, most of the time, is interesting and even fun. School, for a lot of people, is not either very interesting or much fun.

The upside-down school would make study more like work, based on real problems to be solved or real tasks to be done, in groups of mixed ages and different types of ability, all of them useful. Not only would people learn more in such a school, because they would see the point and purpose of what they were doing, but it would give them a better idea of the world they would be entering. Most people's only experience of an organization and of work before the age of 16 is that of a school. If my investigation is anything to go by today's students will leave with a rather strange impression of both an organization and of work.

Other Types Of Intelligence

Society today sieves people in their late teens. The clever ones go on to further studies and qualifications, the rest are left to fend for themselves. We only use one sieve, that of intellectual achievement as measured by examinations. People are interviewed, it is true, by some universities and colleges but you only get to be interviewed if you have passed through that first intellectual sieve.

Upside-down thinking regards this as nonsense. We need more talents than the intellect, important though that is. Talent, we know, has many faces. So does intelligence. Howard Gardner, a professor at the Harvard School of Education took the trouble to classify seven different types of intelligence which, he claims, we can actually measure. Based on his analysis, but stretching it a little, we can in a commonsense way recognize some distinct sorts of intelligence or talent in people, even at a young age.

1. *Analytical intelligence* – the sort we measure in I.Q. tests and in most examinations.
2. *Pattern intelligence* – the ability to see patterns in things and to create patterns. Mathematicians, artists, computer programmers often have this intelligence to a high degree. (It is important to realize that the talents are not connected or

correlated. It is possible to be very intelligent in a pattern sense and to fail all conventional exams.)

3. *Musical intelligence* – some musicians, pop stars, for example, are analytically clever but many are not. Musically intelligent they undoubtedly are.

4. *Physical intelligence* – swimmers, footballers, sports stars of all sorts have this talent in abundance – it is no guarantee of the other talents.

5. *Practical intelligence* – the sort of intelligence that can take a television to bits, put it together again without instructions, but might not be able to spell the names of the parts.

6. *Intra-personal intelligence* – the person, often the quiet one, who is in tune with feelings, their own and others, the poets and the counsellors.

7. *Inter-personal intelligence* – the ability to get on with other people, to get things done with and through others. It is the skill that managers have to have, in addition to one or other of the first two types.

All these intelligences, or talents, we can recognize as having their place in life. If we look around in middle age at the people who are happy and successful we see it is because they have found what they are good at and are doing it. By that stage the first of the intelligences is by no means the most important.

Ironically, all these intelligences are also recognized in British schools but, apart from the first, analytical intelligence, they are collectively grouped under the heading 'out of school activities', and in too many schools there are now no out of school activities.

All the seven intelligences, and there may be more, will be needed even more in the portfolio world towards which we are inching our way. It is crazy, therefore, to use only the first of the intelligences as the criterion for further investment in any individual by society.

The system of universal educational credits would avoid

this blinkered approach. The upside-down school with study as work would also find that it needed to recognize the other intelligences *inside* school hours. Indeed, the upside-down school might usefully make it a point of principle that *every* student should leave school demonstratably successful, in at least one of the intelligences.

There are some signs of change in every country. Learning is increasingly accepted as meaning something more than acquiring knowledge. Capability, competence and social skills are rewarded and recorded in many schools. In Britain many schools use individual Records of Achievements to recognize different forms of success and different types of intelligence. In America, in similar vein, young people are encouraged to see their schooldays as an opportunity to start compiling their 'bios', their lists of accomplishments both inside and outside the classroom. In France they intend that 75 per cent of young people should get their baccalaureat but there will be different *baccalauréats* for different talents.

Education needs, however, to move further and faster if it is going to catch up the future. A system which has in the past allowed more than a third of its members to leave without even one acceptable mark of achievement has to be more de-skilling, particularly for a portfolio world. In that world, self-confidence, a saleable skill or talent and an ability to cope with life and to communicate are critical. Success, of some sort, needs to be part of everyone's early experience. That is why a wider and more formal acceptance of the other types of intelligence is so crucial.

Educational Credits

Education has to be a huge priority for everyone in the world of work that is emerging. It will not be enough to turn a few schools into shamrocks. We have got to do some more fundamental re-framing.

Upside-down thinking suggests that society should think of funding the individual rather than the institution wherever possible, as a way of releasing the motivation to learn in more people and to get the wheel of learning moving universally. If potential undergraduates, for instance, were each given an educational credit voucher to be cashed in at any university or college that would accept them, the institutions would be free to set their own fees, expand or contract as they pleased without reference to university funding councils or whoever. New institutions might be created to cash in on the new markets, whereas before only government could add to the supply. This way the state funds the customer and the supply creates itself.

Upside-down thinking goes on to wonder why it is that everyone has to rush off to college at 18 when so much of what one needs to learn only becomes apparent at a much later age. Furthermore, what logic is it which says that 18 is the age at which to decide that more formal education is appropriate? Indeed, if the numbers in Chapter 2 are even approximately correct we shall need to educate twice as many of each age group up to degree standard, but not necessarily all at once.

One answer would be to give everyone three years' worth of educational credits, to be cashed in at any time in their lives, as long as they could find a licensed college to accept them. The credits would cover the fees, not the grants, so not everyone would be able or want to cash them in, but more would study part-time later in life, more would be supported by firms or by their own savings, more institutions would arise to take advantage of the bigger market. It would be a cheap way for government to increase the supply of graduates, tapping into the ones that were missed in the bulge years of the early 1980s. All they would have to do to maintain quality would be to monitor the standards of institutions through a licensing system, which is already in existence in Britain.

Educational credits have long been a suggestion put forward by the European Community office in Brussels. They need now to be taken more seriously by individual governments. One way to reduce the cost would be to make a one year credit part of any redundancy notice, thus getting organizations to fund some of the scheme.

Upside-down thinking goes on to suggest that three or four consecutive years in one institution is not the only or even the best way to spend a precious three years' worth of credits. It should be possible to spread them out over a longer period or even over different institutions. Transferable course credits, as they have in West Germany, need to become part of our educational tradition if people are going to be able to build up a portfolio of learning, spread over time and over subjects. The Open University in Britain, with its open entry requirements, its credit accumulation scheme and its modular appeal is halfway there. When its approach is followed more widely and its course credits are more widely accepted in other institutions we shall be getting closer to the flexi-education we need for our flexi-lives.

The credit transfer does not have to be confined to formal colleges or universities. The great bulk of study is now taking place inside organizations. Provided this education is up to standard there is no good reason why it should not earn credits for its participants. We may soon expect to see business organizations seeking validation for their executive courses from business schools. The so-called 'consortium MBAs' recently pioneered in Britain, where a group of companies collaborated with a business school to mount a degree programme for their executives, is a move in this direction. It is another way for the upside-down state to get its further education done properly for nothing. Organizations in Britain like the BBC and Hewlett-Packard are taking clever arts graduates and training them, in one year, to be electronics experts. They do it because they have to, but in one sense, why should they *not* have to? Why should we not expect the world of work to educate its own people? The older professions have always done this, others will surely follow.

The Learning Organization

'The Learning Organization' is a term currently in vogue. It is, however, less than obvious what it means except that clearly it is a good thing to strive to be. The model of learning on which this chapter is based gives us some clues.

The learning organization can mean two things, it can mean an organization which learns and/or an organization which encourages learning in its people. It should mean both. As an organization which learns, and which wants its people to learn, it needs to follow the precepts of the theory explained in Chapter 3 of the wheel and its necessary lubricants. In particular:

Asking questions and testing theories

A learning organization needs to have a formal way of asking questions, seeking out theories, testing them and reflecting upon them. Too many organizations are like Action Men or Pragmatists, reacting to events and adapting creatively and opportunistically.

The incoming Director of the Tate Gallery in London in 1988 deliberately set up a series of one-day think-ins with his new staff to answer a whole series of questions ranging from the role of the gallery to how do we fund it and staff it. He used his opportunity as a newcomer to lift the questions, and the possible answers, out of the everyday and to give them a special attention. Other organizations formally review their competitor's work and progress and use the review as a way to start the questions in some off-site top-level gathering. The Japanese are particularly fond of sending senior executives on study visits to competitors in other countries, raising questions and gathering ideas.

More typically, an organization does it in a corporate classroom, inviting a faculty from the world outside to raise issues and pose solutions. This can be an excuse to get stuck in the second stage of the wheel, listening to great theories in response to questions which nobody feels the organization has. These sort of seminars can too easily become corporate comfort pills, 'Thank God, we don't have to take any notice of that stuff since we don't have the illness it is intended for.' More accurately, someone on the staff has the questions and wants to use the experts to sell some answers, but unless all those present have the same questions and the same need to deal with them, nothing at all will happen.

Nor is it any use, of course, delegating the questions and the theories to some groups of scenario planners, corporate planners or even outside consultants. If the key executives feel no ownership of the questions and the theories they will not want to take the risk of testing them. The wheel will have got stuck. The top executives themselves have to be the ones who ask the questions, seek out the ideas, and test the best of them and then, deliberately, take time out to reflect on the results. It is no accident that the most successful corporate leaders give so much time to looking *outside* the organization, or that a leader's job requires so much time spent in *other* people's worlds if he or she is to avoid the dangers of 'group-think', the group that does not ask the uncomfortable questions or look at the uncomfortable ideas.

The wheel of learning cannot be left to chance or to the Chairman thinking in the bathtub. It has to be organized if the organization is to learn. John Harvey-Jones describes, in his book *Making it Happen*, how much time and attention he gave to creating the space for his top people to question, think and learn in his first years as Chairman of ICI.

A proper selfishness

The learning organization is properly selfish, it is clear about its role, its future, has goals and is determined to reach them. That sounds trite and obvious, but it is not that easy in practice. 'To make profits' or 'the bottom line' is not, by itself, a useful way of describing the purpose behind an organization. It does not begin to tell you what to do or what to be. It is akin to an individual saying that he or she wants to be happy. Of course, happiness and profitability is a state devoutly to be wished for but it is not a purpose. If anything, profits are a means and not an end. Without them, purposes are difficult to achieve.

Effective organizations know this now. Japanese corporations have always known it, which has been part of their strength. Their sources of finance know it, too, which sadly is not always the case in Britain and the USA. As in the case of an individual, the questions behind a proper selfishness in an organization are clear:

What are the organization's strengths and talents?
Its weaknesses?
What sort of organization does it want to be?
What does it want to be known for?
How will its success be measured, by whom and when?
How does it plan to achieve it?

The answers, for most organizations, must start with the customer or the client – who are they, what do they need, what do they want, how can we know? Without customers, after all, no organization has the right to exist. The story of the hospital administrator, congratulated on his efficient hospital, who replied, 'Thank you, but you should have seen it before we let the patients in, it was really beautiful then', may be apocryphal but it is all too reminiscent of organizations who seem to exist only for themselves. '*Involutus per se*', to be 'turned in on oneself' said St Augustine, was the worst of sins – *improper* selfishness.

A way of re-framing

The learning organization is constantly re-framing the world and its part in it. Leaders, I have argued earlier, need good conceptual skills. Even when these come with the genes they still need development and exercise. Every organization as it moves towards federalism and large do'nuts needs more leaders everywhere, more re-framing everywhere, not just at the top. Good do'nut definition is all about re-framing, just as the 'what business are we in this year' is also re-framing.

The quality circles in manufacturing organizations are, at their best, examples of re-framing at the shop-floor or office-floor level. They are, actually, the wheel of learning in action, with problems to be raised, ideas suggested, tested and reviewed. They will always work best, however, when the problem can be re-framed.

Quality circles are one example of how some organizations have incorporated re-framing and the learning cycle into their formal organization. Others create temporary think-tanks for their leaders in seminars in resort hotels, others hire consultants (with the attendant dangers of loss of ownership of the result). Once again, it cannot be left to chance.

Re-framing often needs some outside stimulus. Re-framers need to walk in other people's worlds from time to time. It is here that outside conferences, courses and seminars really have their uses, but those attending them should not look for neat answers but only for a stimulus to re-framing. The other worlds of books, of theatre and art and travel, are also good aids to re-framing. They need to be cultivated by a learning organization, not frowned upon as indulgences.

One of the problems of life in the high-pressure core of the shamrock organization is that there is too little time now for walking in other people's worlds. Even holidays can be interrupted, work can be done at home as easily or better than in the office, breakfast and dinners used as an opportunity for meetings, even visits to the opera turned into organization business. The learning organization must therefore make it an *organizational* responsibility to push people into those other worlds lest it be afflicted with a severe case of endemic group-think.

Negative capability

The learning organization must cultivate its negative capability. Disappointment and mistakes are part of change and essential to learning. 'How big a mistake can you now make without them stopping you first?' I asked a young friend who was boasting of his new promotion. I was suggesting that real responsibility entailed the risk of big mistakes. Learning organizations start by giving space, large do'nuts in my language. Large do'nuts mean discretionary space, space which will sometimes be misused. A learning organization will try to turn those mistakes into learning opportunities, not by using them as sticks to beat with but as case-studies for discussion.

Incidental Learning, Alan Mumford calls it, the learning that can be built around incidents in everyone's life and career. To be done without blame, however, and with implied forgiveness, the learning needs to be facilitated not by a boss or supervisor but by a neutral mentor or coach from inside, or, often, from outside the organization. Incidental Learning, properly done, uses the incident to raise the questions which start the wheel of learning. The mentor role will become increasingly important as do'nuts get larger. Properly selfish individuals will, if they are wise, look for their own mentors. Organizations could make this easier by maintaining a list of approved, and paid for, mentors, inside and outside. They will not always be people in great authority, those mentors, and will seldom be one's immediate superior. Mentoring is a skill on its own. Quiet people have it more than loud people; for mentors are able to live vicariously, getting pleasure from the success of others; they are interpreters not theorists, nor action men, best perhaps in the reflective stage of learning, people who are attracted by influence not power.

A list of mentors is one outward symbol of an organization's negative capability and of its endorsement of learning. More of these outward symbols are necessary if learning is going to be seen to be respectable, where time for reflection should be legitimate time. People could have individual educational budgets (in time or money) for their own discretionary self-development. Formal appraisal schemes could be re-formulated as self-development contracts, the language being the important symbol here because 'appraisal' sounds like judgement not help, looking backwards not forwards, smacking of authority not partnership.

The caring organization

Learning organizations want everyone to learn always, and bend over backwards to make that obvious. Large do'nuts, self-development contracts, recognized mentors, outside visits and seminars, incidental learning and corporate forgiveness are part of that. So are more formal arrangements such as tuition reimbursement schemes, as found in most American companies, more opportunities to listen in on higher-level debates as in Japan, projects beyond the immediate job, the public encouragement of questions at all levels, quality circles or their equivalent in study teams everywhere, brainstorming parties around new problems, horizontal careers to open up new possibilities, the encouragement of precocity and initiative even if it may offend, rewards tied to output not to status, to performance not age, constant celebrations of achievement and, above all else, a genuine feeling everywhere of 'unconditional positive regard' for the individual or, in more sensible language, of *care* for the individual.

Care is not a word to be found in many organizational

textbooks, or in books on learning theory, but it should be. Forgiveness is not easy without that unconditional positive regard of the sort we feel for our children, no matter how much we disapprove of their behaviour. People do not take risks with those they do not trust or genuinely care for. Subsidiarity comes from more of that trust and more of that positive regard. Loose, dispersed organizations depend on people liking and trusting each other. A culture of excitement, of question and experiment, of exploration and adventure cannot survive under a reign of fear. That kind of culture cannot be imposed, it can only be encouraged by demonstrations of warmth for all that is good, by celebration, by investment in individuals beyond the bounds of prudence. That kind of encouragement is only possible if one genuinely cares for the people being encouraged.

It is an attitude of mind and it shows in simple ways. Jim, the Manager of Indoor Recreation in a Metropolitan council in the north of Britain, has written a short description of his work for a Local Authority Competition on management. He called it 'My Love affair with Change'. He described one incident out of many,

'I should have known we were onto a winner with the staff there. They always made people welcome even management. All they needed was attention, encouragement and freedom. But it became apparent after a meeting of supervisors of all pools.

'I hadn't been in the Swimming Session for too long and we had begun to meet regularly to talk and listen to each other (that's the best way I could think of putting it).

'The supervisors complained that they never had any money to spend ... so I gave them £500 for each pool. The two supervisors at this pool could decide how this money was spent.

'Some bought audio equipment, another bought an external sign and had information leaflets printed. The supervisors at one pool didn't spend their money. At the end of the year they wrote to me saying the interest was worth £50 and it was to go towards their cutbacks for the year.'

Little things and an attitude of mind – attention, encouragement, and genuine care and freedom – add up to a culture of learning, in a learning organization in love with change. It will, however, be more difficult to maintain, this culture of learning, in organizations when many people will be rather temporary inhabitants, passing through in the pursuit of their own careers. It is hard to give as much genuine care to your tenant as to your child who is yours for life. Japanese corporations, with their tradition of life-time employment at least for their core workers, made it easier to create the kind of culture and care for the individual's growth which learning thrives on. We cannot, however, afford to go the Japanese way nor do our Western individuals want that sense of permanent commitment or bondage, and even in Japan the system is beginning to erode.

The fact, however, that it will be more difficult in the shamrock, federal organization only means that it will not happen naturally. The learning organization has to be worked for, consciously. Most sensibly, and practically, it can start by getting rid of the *blocks* to change.

These blocks can be quite effective. Organizations know them well, and use them. Rosabeth Moss Kanter studied a range of large American corporations and reported the news about change in her book *The Change Masters*. She came up with ten rules for stifling initiative:

1. Regard any new idea from below with suspicion – because it is new and because it is from below.
2. Insist that people who need your approval to act first go through several other levels of management to get their signatures.
3. Ask departments or individuals to challenge and criticize each other's proposals.
4. Express your criticisms freely and withhold your praise.

(That keeps people on their toes.) Let them know they can be fired at any time.

5. Treat problems as a sign of failure.

6. Control everything carefully. Count anything that can be counted, frequently.

7. Make decisions to reorganize or change policies in secret and spring them on people unexpectedly (that also keeps people on their toes).

8. Make sure that any request for information is fully justified and that it isn't distributed too freely (you don't want data to fall into the wrong hands).

9. Assign to lower-level managers, in the name of delegation and participation, responsibility for figuring out how to cut back, lay off or move people around.

10. Above all, never forget that you, the higher-ups, already know everything important about this business.

The learning organization needs to break every one of these commandments, frequently.

9 An Upside-Down Society

The Upside-Down State

When Eisenhower was President of Columbia University in New York, before he became President of the USA, he received a deputation from the faculty. Could he, they asked, please use his authority to stop the students walking over the grass in the main quadrangle.

'Why do they walk on the grass?' he asked.

'Because it is the easiest way to get from the main entrance to the central hall.'

'If that's the way they are going to go,' he said, 'then cut a pathway there.' Problem solved.

There is, sometimes, little point in trying to stand in the way of what is happening. It is often better to recognize the inevitable and make it work for you. The changing pattern of work is one of those tides in the affairs of men and women which needs to be channelled, for it will not, cannot, be blocked or dammed. This book is not about politics, but if work is changing so much of our life so radically then it is bound also to have its impact on government and on the rules of society. Government, too, needs to recognize that the changes do make a difference, that more than a marginal adjustment is required, that discontinuity demands some re-thinking and re-framing.

The Henley Centre in Britain, in its 1988 report on Teleworking suggests, for instance, that gasoline stations will lose business along with the railways as commuting declines, that second cars will become unnecessary, road congestion will ease and that the greater availability of time for working (without travelling) might lower the rate of inflation by 0.7 per cent. House prices might even out as people have more freedom to choose where they live and a lot of office cleaners would lose their jobs.

All that however is only the tip of the iceberg. The implications go much deeper than the possible effects of telecommuting. For the past 100 years and more the work organization has been of great use to governments of every political persuasion. The organization has been the way in which wealth has been distributed to the population, in their wage packets or salary cheques. The organization has been, therefore the natural and convenient way to collect taxes and to implement economic policy and to plan resources. If everyone has a job in an organization then the world is easier to control. At the very least we know where most of them are, and where most of them will have to live.

Similarly, organizations have been the easiest route for spending government money. It is easier to pay hospitals to help sick people than to pay the sick to find the hospitals, easier to pay schools or universities en bloc than to pay individuals to go to the schools, easier to run your own railways, coal mines or postal services than to leave it to others. Of course, there are ideological reasons for keeping vital services in government control but it cannot be completely accidental that the enthusiasm for governments to own and control so much coincided with the same fashion in organizations everywhere. 'If you want to control it, own it' was the message in every business in the 1960s and 1970s. Integration was the smart word – horizontal integration, vertical integration or both together. Buy your suppliers, buy your customers, buy your competitors if you can. That way your world is more yours. It was only natural that governments should hear the same message.

It was, as we have seen, an expensive message. Organizations now think differently. Shamrocks and federations are more economic even if they are more difficult to control.

The new fashion will not leave governments unscathed. They, too, will find that it makes sense to work out their core tasks, to do those well with the best people, and to contract out the rest for others to do. To call this privatisation is to miss a large part of the point. It is not all, or perhaps even mostly about ideology, it is about the most effective and efficient way to run organizations. The shamrocks of the state may be expected to spread for quite a while, nor will it be easy to reverse the trend.

More fundamental, however, is the way work is moving outside the organization. More fee work, more telecommuting, more self-employment makes it more difficult for the government to collect prices, influence earnings or manage welfare. Self-employed people cannot by law or logic be unemployed, only broke. Nor do the self-employed ever really retire, they only slow down. Unemployment and retirement begin to be technical terms only, not ones that usefully describe the human condition. So it is that a government can proudly announce a fall in unemployment while the opposition may simultaneously claim that the real number of people wanting work is rising. They are talking about different things. Inevitably, now, government will have increasingly to deal direct with individuals rather than with organizations, will have to re-think the categories it puts people into, and find some new ways to organize the collection and distribution of wealth if the organization cannot do it for them. The time of discontinuous change needs some upside-down thinking.

The shamrocks and federations of the state
The British Civil Service is devolving a large part of itself into agencies. Railways may become Track Authorities, with private companies running competing train services along those tracks, rather like an Airport Authority. The BBC may be whittled down to a centrally funded news service with all other programmes contracted out to small

documentary and film companies. The mail service in each country may be confined to the main track routes between big cities with franchisees bidding for the right to deliver the mail to our doorsteps, or more likely, to our private box numbers.

It could go farther still. In the USA prisons are put out on private contract, rather like security for the plant. Maybe parts of the defence contract could also be sub-contracted. Schools, as we shall see, could become brokers in education, the intermediaries between learners and a whole range of potential suppliers. Motorways and inner city streets could all become toll roads with automatic charging from strips in the road to meters in every car, allowing individual businesses to bid for building and running roads and motorways.

These are the signs of the principles of subsidiarity and the inverted do'nut creeping into government. Governments are doing what organizations are doing – re-thinking their core function. It should be no surprise that they often conclude that it is the job of the core to set and to maintain standards, to establish a framework and to choose the contractors but *not* to try to do the job themselves. If business organizations increasingly find that what they can most usefully do is to identify the essential core of the do'nut (the standards), to define the outer rim of discretion (the framework), to select the people, and to leave the rest to their individual initiatives, then governments will in time follow the fashion and start to do likewise. They already are.

They will not, of course, pay tribute to organizational thinking when they start to reform their ways. That would be unnatural. They will claim it always as a victory for their particular brand of politics for it is not difficult to make organizational effectiveness an essential plank in the political philosophies of either left and/or right. What today is called 'privatisation' to emphasize the diminished role of government as operator, could equally well be called 'democratization' to emphasize the return of choice to the client or consumer. No doubt in time it will be called just that. In the meantime I shall continue to believe that the laws of organizations are ultimately inexorable.

A National Income Scheme
Education is critical if we are going to give more, if not all, of our citizens the ability to work and live in this new world. But education on its own will not be enough. We have to find other ways of 'empowering' people as individuals. A national income scheme is one possibility.

The national income is conventionally the income of the nation as calculated by the statistical service. Upside-down thinking suggests that it ought instead to be defined as the income which every citizen should receive from the state. The idea has been around for a long time and has been given various names – a social wage, a national dividend, a citizen's salary, a basic income, but it has never been thought practical or, indeed, necessary as long as most people were guaranteed their income through their job.

Things are different now. People lose their job through no fault of their own. Ten per cent of the working population with no paid work at all is a lot of people. Others do not get included in the ten per cent but are still impoverished, like many of the self-employed. In order to get financial support from the state you have to classify yourself as old, unable to get work or poor. It is demeaning, people feel, in a free society.

A free society, and a rich society in comparative terms, ought to be able to guarantee its people enough money to pay for food, clothes and heating, as well as the free education and free health care which it already gives them. Upside-down thinking suggests that instead of paying cash to the needy few we should pay it to everyone and then claw it back progressively for those that *don't* need it.

Put more idealistically the argument is that as citizens we

are both entitled to an income from our collective property, our society, as well as obligated to pay a portion of our individual earnings for the maintenance of that society. *All* of us have the entitlement and the obligation.

It would work like this, at its most simple. Everyone would receive a weekly or a monthly income from the state. It could be smaller at 16 and 76 than at 36 or 46, to match the changing curve of spending. That income is never taken away from you, you do not lose it when you start earning - the penalty under the present system which discourages so many unemployed from re entering the labour market. Instead you start to repay it when you start to earn. That repayment tax might start at 60 per cent and would then *fall*, not rise, as you earned more, giving even more incentive to keep on working. The repayment scheme would be in addition to income tax which would not, however, normally start to bite until the repayment tax was very small.

The results might be interesting:

— Because everyone would receive the national income there would be no need for people to classify themselves as unemployed or retired in order to get money. Those words would simply disappear, and with them the categories of people. More people would just be living off their dividends as the people of property have always done. Now anyone could do it, in a small way.

— Because the national income, although very basic, would cover essentials, it would make sense to do some extra work quite cheaply because one would keep about half of it. The marginal cost of labour would therefore tend to fall, more jobs would be worth doing, we should start to price some work back into existence, particularly at the low-skilled manual end where it is most needed.

— Because there would be more money circulating at the bottom end of the income scale there would be more consumers; therefore, in the end, more work making and doing the things those consumers want; (if we don't import them all of course).

There are problems, of course. Giving money to people does not necessarily mean that they will spend it sensibly. Some will waste it on booze, drugs or horses and *still* come to the state for support. Hopefully, they would be a small minority but they would be there and something would have to be done for them by someone. Would we consider that they had any further call on society, or would we leave it to charitable organizations to help any who cannot help themselves?

It would be hard to get started. This excuse is often made but I am not convinced. It is, after all, only the same amount of money being circulated in a different way. It would help if it were done in conjunction with the next piece of upside-down thinking.

Zero income tax

Upside-down thinking goes beyond a truly national income. Why have any income tax at all? It only raises the cost of labour and therefore the cost of the product and so ultimately helps to price more work/jobs out of existence.

Income tax has been, of course, the easy way to collect taxes, even though it was originally introduced as a temporary measure. It won't be easy for much longer when only half the working population and less than 20 per cent of the total population will be on the permanent payroll. Self-employment tax is much more difficult to assess and to collect and will get more so as more people become self-employed.

Income tax, however, produces half of the country's revenue with expenditure or indirect taxation (sales tax, customs duties, car tax etc) producing the other half. We would therefore have to double our expenditure taxes, or tax more things like food and books if income tax were abolished. This, it is argued, would be too regressive, i.e.

bear down too heavily on the poorest. However, if the national income scheme were in operation this argument would not be so crucial. The poorest would still pay proportionately more of their income but would be recompensed through their national income cheques.

A doubling of expenditure taxes might, however, be very inflationary since the prices of everything on the retail price index would automatically increase. It would only be seriously inflationary, however, if it were done at a stroke, as Britain did in the first year of Mrs Thatcher's government. A gradual progressive move towards a zero rate of income tax and doubled expenditure taxes might avoid the inflationary repercussions.

The implications would, again, be interesting:

— Any tax reliefs on, for instance, housing loans or pensions would progressively be reduced to zero, reducing the price of houses and directing more savings elsewhere, perhaps into more productive investments.
— As there would be no further point in people trying to conceal or reduce their apparent income, the workload of accountants and revenue officials would fall dramatically.
— Expenditure taxes as the only form of taxation would mean that you only pay tax when you spend money. Savings would therefore be automatically tax exempt, tempting people to save more.
— All forms of 'perks' would lose their rationale as tax-effective ways of paying people, making 'clean cash' contracts more sensible.

The switch from income to expenditure taxes will never happen overnight, but it could and should happen gradually. It needs to, because income tax will become progressively harder to collect, with the likely result that, the rate will rise rather than decrease, putting up the cost of salaries in the core and putting even more pressure on organizations to reduce the numbers of core employees. It is a spiral without end. We should deliberately try to go the other way, even if at first it seems perverse.

Part-time professionals
As the world gets more complicated we inevitably acquire more experts, in every field. We have already noted that sixty per cent of new jobs will be professional or managerial. Who will fill them? Technology will not make their jobs any easier but it could make them better. Computer diagnosis in every doctor's surgery will not remove the doctor but will enable him or her to be a *better* doctor. It will be the same for lawyers, architects, consultant engineers – for all our experts.

Professionals will be in short supply; professionals will be better equipped, professionals will, quite clearly, be very busy. One suspects that they will be the one group of people who will greatly exceed the 50,000 hour norm for the job. They will need help, particularly with the ancillary areas of counselling, of follow-up, of semi-skilled assistance. Upside-down thinking suggests that we should treat this as an opportunity not as a problem.

Can we not devise more ways to use the intelligence and the experience of people in their Third Age to help in these ancillary areas? As a part of their portfolio it would be of interest to many people in their fifties to have a part-time relationship with a doctor's practice, with a school, with a solicitor or in a parish. Some of this already happens: there are counsellors in some surgeries, teaching assistants in some primary schools. We will need more of them as the full-time professionals get busier, and they need to be given a more formal status and the necessary training.

It would not necessarily be expensive. Many would do it for free, for the chance of the training and the opportunity to contribute. Others would expect only part-time pay for part-time work. A lot of the time would be spent in adding a human touch to the gadgetry and technology that will increasingly become part of all professional services, and in listening and in explaining – things for which the expert often has neither the time nor the inclination.

Upside-down thinking would like these roles to be properly certificated and licensed, with required training procedures, rather than regarded as ad hoc voluntary help. In this way the public would feel reassured and the helper would feel properly recognized and qualified. It would enrich the portfolio of many a middle-aged person and enrich our society.

There are, to take one example, hundreds if not thousands of churches in communities which can no longer justify a full-time priest. They are now served by one man, or just occasionally now one woman, driving frantically from church to church with not much time for anything else, a visiting religious impresario, not at all the role for which he was trained. There must be many who would be eager, with proper training, to serve as part-time priest to their small community, licensed to that community only, and drawing on the expertise of the full-time priest, in the neighbouring town when it is needed. The concept exists, it is called the non-stipendiary ministry, meaning unpaid, but it is still seen as the assistant ministry. Upside-down thinking would argue that it should be the main ministry, a truly local ministry, served and advised by a small full-time core located in regional centres – the shamrock again.

It is, however, the professional caring services which are going to be overstretched in the new society as people live longer and more on their own. We will need more and better homes for old people, delivery services for them, information and home counselling services, dial-a-meal and dial-a-ride services, perhaps even dial-a-nurse. There will not be enough full-time professionals to man these services.

Part-time professionals in their Third Age could be a great help.

Time pay not money pay
If people are plentiful but money is scarce why not pay some people in time rather than money?

It was Stephen Bragg's idea originally, when he was Chairman of a Health Authority in Britain. Money was short in the health service. Consultants as they get older get progressively more expensive, therefore his Authority could afford fewer of them, getting older, while younger would-be consultants queued up, champing at the bit. Why not, he argued, pay all consultants the same, but require less time from them as they got promoted? They could use that time to work outside the system for money, or inside for no money, or they could use it to go fishing. The Authority would be able to afford more consultants, working the younger ones harder, but retaining the wisdom and exper-tise of the older ones. It was real upside-down thinking and, predictably, was never taken seriously.

The idea, however, becomes relevant when organizations want to shift people in their core from an energy role to a wisdom role. Expressed conventionally it often feels like demotion. Expressed as time pay in place of money pay it has another ring to it.

It is also a way of making sense of one's portfolio. Some things are done for money, some for love or goodwill, some for the discretionary time they give you. I write books. They don't, unfortunately, make much money. I know that but still I do it, partly because that sort of work forces me to set aside large chunks of discretionary time, to pay myself in time not money. Others take care to keep three days a week free of formal commitments, to make sure that they have 'free time', paying themselves, deliberately, in time.

One can give people time in other ways – time for education, time for children and a family, time for self-development as well, of course, as time for holidays. People in the core may well value time more than money in their pay packets. It is the sort of upside-down thinking which more organizations will cultivate as they look for ways to keep the best people in their cores.

There is, it seems to me, a real possibility that more and more of the most talented people in society may choose to exchange an executive role for a portfolio life quite early in their careers, preferring more control over their time even if combined with a more perilous financial future, preferring, in other words, to balance money pay with time pay. If that occurred, then our organizations would be in danger of becoming the reservoirs of the second best – not a good omen for their effectiveness.

Paying people in time rather than money, particularly towards the end of their job-life, would do something to put the curve of lifetime earnings more in line with the lifetime spending curve. It has always seemed odd that people got most money when they needed it least, in their late fifties and sixties, having scraped and scrimped in earlier years to raise a family. In a sensible world earnings would peak in the forties and would then scale down not up, replaced by more of that discretionary time which was so scarce before.

The Upside-Down Game

Upside-down thinking is like brainstorming. It is easy to think of violent objections to every idea. It is easy but unwise. It is unwise because that will stop the idea in its tracks, before it has had a chance to stretch itself, to get nudged into shape and, perhaps, to speak other and better ideas. It is easy to listen to a new idea and say 'Why?' It is more exciting to listen and say 'Why not?'

The ideas in this chapter are not intended to be a carefully worded prospectus for action. They are here to provoke, to suggest that the world does not have to be run as it has traditionally been run. Looking at things upside-down, or back to front, or inside out, is a way of stimulating the imagination, of spurring our creativity in an Age of Unreason when things are not going to go on working as they have been working, whether we like it or not.

It is a game, in a way, but a game with a purpose. If life *is* changing as fundamentally as I think it is, then creativity in our social order will be of immense importance. The status quo cannot be the way forward, nor will the status quo, slightly amended, be the best way forward. Then the Mancur Olsen argument comes into play, that the social order only changes when war, calamity or revolution upsets the status quo.

The danger of doing nothing is that the underclass (that new alarming word), excluded from the world we are moving into, takes its own initiatives, substituting terrorism for politics and bombs for votes, as their way of turning the world upside-down.

I hope we can find another way. It has been the British and American way to change things by a process of case law, of case law made into the new fashion, and, ultimately, the new social order. It is in a way a form of gradualism. Change so gentle that you do not take alarm. That way the censorship of literature in books or on stage was watered down until it has almost disappeared, that way homosexuality ceased to be a crime, that way divorce became a part of the new society, that way, I hope, smoking will disappear from public places, drunkenness from our roads and violence from our screens.

Ideas become fashion as a way to change. It is slow, but, as I argued in the beginning, ideas can change the world. I would like to see the upside-down game become fashionable in those quarters which affect to control or influence our social order. I would encourage the think-tanks of right and left to think boldly rather than too practically, the parties of opposition to challenge fundamentals not details, academics and teachers to encourage more why's? and why nots? in their students, rather than what? and how?

A changing world needs new ideas. The more there are the more used we shall get to them. Thinking the unthinkable is a way of getting the wheel of learning moving, in society as much as in individuals. If the upside-down game caught on, we might be on the move. It is because I am convinced that mankind is essentially a *learning* creature that I am, at heart, an optimist. I see the problems ahead as the necessary triggers for learning, and therefore for changing. I worry only that we won't worry enough, that like the boiling frog in Chapter 1, we shall continue to adapt ourselves to the changing scene until we boil ourselves alive.

We need more 'unreasonable people' who want to change their world not adapt to it, and who want to challenge orthodoxy rather than rationalize away its inconvenient bits. In the end it's a question of belief. I believe that we are the inheritors of a most interesting creation (however it occurred). It is our responsibility to make it better, not just to survive. I believe that holds true for organizations, who have a duty to do more than survive, for governments and for every individual. We cannot leave it to 'them' whoever we think 'they' are. In an Age of Unreason leaving it to 'them' would be foolhardy.

If, however, it is gradual change rather than violent change which we want, change by case law and by new ideas made fashionable, then it is crucial that those who might be 'they' get involved in some of the re-framing and the upside-down thinking. If they do not see change as an opportunity for everyone they will only invite violent change by those excluded.

This book, for that reason, is not about *un*employment but about employment, for only those in work can in the end improve the world for those without work. This book, for that same reason, is not addressed to the underclass, whoever they are, or to the undereducated but to those in positions of responsibility and respectability because only they can change things for those outside, *if* they have a care to.

My concern is that a world where the individual is left even more to his or her own devices, as more of work and life moves outside the institutions of society, could be a world designed for selfishness, and a selfishness which might not always be 'proper' in the sense of Chapter 8. Kingman Brewster, once President of Yale, then US Ambassador to Britain, once memorably asked a gathering of the British great and good 'Who are the trustees of our future?' There was an embarrassed mumble but no clear response. The question still holds good and my answer is that it has to be all of us, at least all of us who are capable of reading a book like this, and who have a concern for the world our children and our grandchildren will grow up in.

We may not, individually, be able to make their world safer from nuclear war, or to preserve the rain forests better, or to keep the ozone layer intact, but, as I argued at the beginning, it is often the little things of life which matter most, the ways we work and love and play, the ways we relate to people and the manner in which we spend our days as well as our money. These things we can affect. We do not have to accept them as they are. The Age of Unreason is inevitably going to be something of an exploration, but exploring is at the heart of learning, and of changing and of growing. This is what I believe and this is what gives me hope.

Epilogue

The world that our parents knew is not the world we live in today; nor is our world any sure guide to the way our children will live and love and work. We live in an Age of Unreason when we can no longer assume that what worked well once will work well again, when most assumptions can legitimately be challenged.

One thing however is clear: institutions will be less important. More of us will spend more of our lives outside formal organizations. 'What,' I said to the Chairmen of some large financial institutions, 'will your executives and your brokers be doing between the ages of fifty and eighty when, assuredly, they will not be working for you or with you?' 'It's a good question,' they acknowledged, 'and one we ought to look at sometime.' By the time they do many of those 50-year-olds will have moved on and out.

'I have ever hated all nations, professions and communities, and all my love is towards people,' said the poet Pope, 'but principally I hate and detest that animal called man, although I heartily love John, Peter, Thomas and so forth.' He would have been pleased with the way things are going, even with the chance to add a feminine name or two to the catalogue, for this is an age when individual differences will be important, both inside and outside organizations. The successful organization will be built around John and Peter, Mary and Catherine, not around anonymous human resources, while in the world outside the organization there will be no collective lump to hide under. We shall have to stand each behind our own name tag.

It should suit countries like Britain rather well. Condemned for decades for the ineffectiveness of much of her industry, Britain has always been renowned and even celebrated for her journalism, for her television and her theatre, for skills of finance and consultancy, of architecture and civil engineering, for medicine and surgery, for design and photography and fashion. These are all by-line occupations, meaning that the individual is encouraged to put his or her name to the work. They are all occupations where the organizations are more like a network than a pyramid, where hierarchy is minimal and individual talent of great importance. As more of industry and more of commerce become by-line occupations they will fit more naturally into the individual ethos of Britain and, indeed, of most Americans. The mass organizations of 'hands' and 'resources' never worked too well in the old democracies of either nation. It will be interesting to see how long they continue to work effectively in the newer democracies of Asia.

A society of individual differences, however, has its problems as well as its undoubted opportunities. Liberty, or the right to be different, and equality have always been the two proud goals of democracy. Unfortunately it has always proved difficult to have both at the same time. If people are encouraged to be different they will not end up equal and if they are to be kept level they will have to have their liberty curtailed; nor is equality of opportunity, normally defined as the right to go to school and hospital, quite the same thing as a full equality. A society founded on individualism could fall apart without the glue of fraternity that the French revolutionists added to liberty and equality; fraternity, or the awareness that there are others who are as important as oneself.

The Paradox Of Choice

People who are free to choose may choose wrongly. This is

the age-old paradox. Sin is the other side of freedom's coin. A world without sin would be a world without choice.

All the forces described in this book seem designed to set the individual free to be more truly himself or herself. Choice is multiple for the fortunate ones. They can choose when to work, at home or in the office: what to eat, with irradiated foods coming fresh from all corners of the world; what to buy via electronic catalogues. They can choose to live richly or thinly in a material sense and even, perhaps, when to die. Within society we may expect the abundance of choice to lead to the erosion of any one dominant set of values. No longer will we see some seeking to set or change the rules while others, the majority, wait to keep the rules they set. 'Anything (or almost anything) goes' will be the message of the next decade. It will be increasingly acceptable to do your own thing provided that thing does not interfere with the choices of too many others. NIMBY (Not In My Backyard) has always become the plea or bleat of those who seek, at the same time, to promote individual liberty and to defend their own islands of privacy, words once again heralding a change of tune.

Achievement and contentment in this society will have many different facets. It could be called a tolerant society, but it could also be a very fragmented society as an individualism rooted in personal achievement and material success replaces the mixture of institutional paternalism and dependency which we grew up in – good news for the strong but not for the weak. Choice, in the end, is only good news for all if everyone has enough to choose from, enough information and enough inner resources. To put it more paradoxically, a society dedicated to the enrichment and enhancement of the self will only survive and certainly will only prosper if its dominant ethic is the support and encouragement of others. Proper selfishness is rooted in unselfishness.

There is a real possibility that the generation now in their thirties, the first generation to experience the full range of choice, may use it to opt out of leadership roles in business and society. For the talented ones a portfolio life on the edges of organizations can be personally fulfilling, free and life-enhancing, but this might condemn organizations to be comprised of the second best and who then will run society? On the other hand, if the leadership roles are going to the talented ones, but also ones who want those roles for their own satisfaction rather than for the good of others, life will become a collection of private courts and courtiers – great if you are in, dismal and bleak if you are outside.

Choice in relationships now means that the extended family is not a collection of aunts, uncles and cousins, but of step-parents and half brothers and sisters, or of step-brothers and sisters with no blood connection at all. The courts may take care of the custody of the very young but who will be responsible for an ageing step-grandmother, or for the lonely sibling fallen on hard times? There are some who hope that new communities, sharing their homes or their workplaces rather than their parentage, will replace the old networks of the family which were so often riven with secret jealousies and ancient feuds. My own fear is that in the end shared bricks are not so reliable as shared blood, that these communities of common interest thrive as long as the interests are common, but fall apart when the interests diverge. Choice can seem a hollow mockery when someone is old and cold and poor; individual freedom can easily mean freedom not to care.

Organizations, for their part, need to think about *their* responsibilities in the midst of the pressures to maintain their flexibility and their freedom of choice. Who, for instance, will train and re-train the contract workers if the organization chooses not to? Education and training definitely increase choice for those educated and thereby give them passports to move to greener pastures but is this really a valid reason for *not* training one's executives? In the past it has been, and in many industries today it is still the plaint of the bigger institutions that they lose their best people as soon as they have trained them and are therefore tempted to turn poachers like the rest. Who then will train the game they want to poach? If organizations continue to think that way then choice will become the enemy of progress. Too much emphasis on organizational choice, on flexibility, can look like a lack of commitment to one's people, inviting a lack of commitment in return. Selfishness breeds selfishness.

Governments, in the meantime, having discovered that the market, the mechanism of choice, liberates initiative and penalizes inefficiency, are tempted to leave all to self-regulating choice. That would be dangerous. Markets do not look much beyond tomorrow, or at least next year. Markets are inherently selfish, disinclined to make investments whose outcomes cannot be precisely predicted or whose benefits cannot be claimed in advance. Basic research, for instance, in new sciences and new technologies has to be an article of faith. Who could predict in advance that the Science Research Council's investment in tracking down the structure of DNA at Cambridge would result in the whole new industry of biotechnology? The education of the next generation, too, has to be an act of faith. Left to individual parents and competing schools it would soon become a vocational rat-race for the few rather than a platform for growth for the many. Japan's government sees it as its responsibility, on behalf of the nation, to put national resources behind an infrastructure of creativity, building a new technopolis in nineteen locations and giving priority, in funding basic research and development, to seven emerging industry sectors. These long-term investments cannot be left to the chance and the choice of individual firms.

When Kingman Brewster asked who were to be the trustees of our future, his point was that governments tend naturally to think short-term and that a national consciousness is needed which makes it permissible to spend our money today for the benefit of grandchildren yet unborn. It would be a reversal of the tradition that it makes good economic sense to borrow from those grandchildren to boost our standard of living today. Market forces will not produce the wherewithals or the political will to tackle the problems of the ozone layer and our possibly melting climate, yet if the Netherlands and East Anglia are not to be submerged in 50 years' time someone must start spending now. That decision requires choice to be exercised by a few on behalf of the many, with the consent of the many – leadership on a big scale.

The New Ethic

In a world of individualism the dominant ethic can so easily become 'What harms no one is OK', or 'What the others do and get away with has to be all right', or even 'If no one knows then you're fine.' At the height of the insider trading scandals of 1987 a leading London banker called insider trading 'a victimless crime', implying that it was more a legal nicety than a sin, rather like taking an extra bottle of whisky through the customs. What is wrong, some athletes say, with the odd drug to boost your stamina – it harms no one save yourself. What is wrong with drawing welfare and doing work on the side, the state can afford it. If that ethic were to prevail then any attempt by governments or organizations to spend money today for benefit in 30 years' time, or to spend more of our money on other people would be futile; voters and shareholders and employees would shout them down.

The new freedoms and the new choices will only survive if those who exercise them take time to look over their shoulders, if they genuinely have a care for others as well as for themselves, others beyond their families and their own institutions. Just as businesses today invest in their local communities out of a sense of enlightened self-interest (good communities mean, in the end, better recruits and better customers) so, too, it is in the long-term interest of us all to make sure that choices are not rationed in our society because any rationing of choice might cause it to self-destruct. It is, however, for companies and individuals a calculation that has to be built on faith instead of genuflecting to the spirit of the times, talking the language of proper selfishness.

We need a new religion to save us, or at least a new fashion. Fraternity, the care for others as much as for oneself, must be our guiding ethic. First learn to love yourself, then your neighbour, but don't forget the neighbour. Hubris, the Greeks called it, when overweening pride, or excessive enthusiasm for your own achievements, aroused the irritation, even envy of the gods. Nemesis, or downfall, would follow. It was a way of putting a moral embargo on improper selfishness. It can't be done by laws, or by institutions, or by taxes, for fraternity is one thing that cannot be contracted out or outsourced. It is a core value, and it is established by the example of the people at the core, by the new élites, the fortunate ones.

The signs are not all that encouraging, but I am hopeful. Conspicious consumption, German cars, the electronic gadgetry, houses that cost more than most people's lifetimes' earnings, those are often the outward and visible signs of greed made respectable. When a company chairman, better nameless, boosts his salary by 37 per cent while his company's profits declined by 7 per cent, and sees no reason for explanation or apology, it can seem that private exploitation of public responsibility has become the norm.

On the other hand there is:

— The Bob Geldof effect. More people, particularly young people, are prepared to give to good causes. More companies

recognize that good causes have a legitimate claim on their budgets and give less grudgingly.
— The willing taxpayer. Nearly 80 per cent of Britons, in many surveys, would like to pay more taxes if these resulted in better education, health care and social welfare.
— The young crusaders. Many young people want to spend at least part of their youth working overseas or helping out in places of adversity. The knowledge that they themselves will probably never be destitute seems to give them a new sense of freedom.
— The Third Age. As more and more middle-aged people discover that there is life beyond retirement, with real work to do, their values often shift. Having proved themselves in their work they now want to improve the lot of others – by helping in education, in voluntary organizations, in sports and community associations. Helping others becomes a way of giving new meaning to themselves.
— Institutional tithing. More organizations are encouraging their employees to lend their talents and/or their time to charitable causes, often in the firms' own time, sometimes through secondment, sometimes by corporate support for individual initiatives.

More needs to happen.

True fulfilment is, I believe, vicarious. We get our deepest satisfaction from the fulfilment and growth and happiness of others. It takes time, often a lifetime, to realize this. Parents know it well, as do teachers, great managers and all who care for the downtrodden and unfortunate. We need to give more public expression of what is a deep human characteristic, so that we are not ashamed to be seen to care for others as well as for ourselves, for the future of all as much as for our own, for everyone's environment as well as our own.

My hope is that as more people have more time outside organizations they will discover that portfolios are always enriched by work done for others. I believe that the intensification and the rationing of paid work will, ironically perhaps, encourage more gift work or unpaid work as people realize that it is the 'contribution' element in work which they miss most, and that contribution can be found in a wide variety of work, most of it outside organizations.

My hope is that as more people can choose where to live they will live in places more like villages than cities, places where your neighbours have a name and a face, where their concerns gradually become part of your concerns. It is always more difficult to care for strangers, or for people in the abstract. In a society of smaller communities there should be fewer strangers and more time to stand and talk as well as stare.

My hope is that life is now the right way round. Our wants are arranged in a hierarchy, as Abraham Maslow pointed out long ago, or, to put it more simply, life is largely a matter of crossing things off the list until you get to the bits that are really quintessentially 'you'. Success, money and achievement should now, to many, come earlier, leaving them free to be different while there is still time and energy. In the past, there was neither the time nor the energy – too many died without discovering their full portfolio of possibilities.

My hope is that a society of differences will produce many models for success. Achievement will not be measured simply in terms of money and possessions, but by creativity in the arts, by social invention, by lives of dedication to the care of others, by political leadership in small places as well as great, by writing and acting and music of quality. We need to make sure that the whole variety is honoured, by press and politicians alike.

My hope is that our various religions and faiths will be more outward-looking than inward-looking, realizing that to strive towards a heaven, or something like it, in this world, is the best guarantee of one in the next world, wherever and whatever that may be. Britain's countryside is dotted with ancient churches. They are important symbols, but they should be symbols not of spiritual escapism but of God's and man's involvement in the world around them.

My hope, finally, is in the nature of man himself, and particularly of woman. I believe that a lot of our striving after the symbols and levers of success is due to a basic insecurity, a need to prove ourselves. That done, grown up at last, we are free to stop pretending. I am conscious that we each have our quota of original sin but I also believe in original goodness. The people I admire most have grown up soonest and become their own people. That seems to happen more easily outside the constricting roles of institutions. The world I see emerging with its looser organizations, has many threats and many dangers but it should allow more people to stop pretending much earlier in their lives. If that is so, then the Age of Unreason may become an Age of Greatness.

For Reading and Reference

I have mentioned several authors and books in the text. These books and articles have influenced me and are all worth reading if you want to take any of the subjects a little farther. I list them here with a brief description.

Chapter One:
Olsen, M. *The Rise and Decline of Nations.* Yale University Press 1982.
    A penetrating study of how and why societies freeze up or change.
The Cookham Group. *Headlines 2000.* Hay Management Consultants 1988.
    A look at the world ahead by a group of young executives, sponsored by the Hay Group. Readable and thought-provoking.
Jones, B. *Sleepers Wake!* Wheatsheaf Books 1982.
    A warning directed at Australia to re-think her ways of work and life. Very pertinent to Britain.

Chapter Three:
Kinsman, F. *The Telecommuters.* John Wiley and Sons 1987.
    A glance at one part of the world of the future, built around case studies of organizations who have tried it. Readable and eye-opening.
Hakim, C. 'Homeworking in Britain', and Baran, B., 'Office Automation and Women's Work', both in *Pahl, R.E. (ed) On Work.* Blackwell 1988.
    Pahl's book of readings is a bit academic but provides a broad canvas of thought and research on the way work has changed over the centuries. A lot of the articles are by women. An interesting backcloth to this book.

Chapter Four:
Naisbitt, J. *Reinventing the Corporation.* Warner Books 1985.
    An anecdotal but upside-down view of corporate changes in America. A follow-up to the same author's best-selling *Megatrends* of 1982.

Chapter Five:
Deming, W.E. *Out of the Crisis.* Cambridge University Press 1986.
    The latest book by the greatest of the quality gurus. Important reading for managers.
Zuboff S. *In the Age of the Smart Machine.* Heinemann Professional Publishing 1988.
    An interesting but rather academic examination of the way the computer changes the notions of work and power in organizations.

Bennis, W. & Nanis, B. *Leaders*. Harper & Row 1986.
   Best read for its revealing description of interviews with a range of American leaders in all types of organizations followed up by Bennis' *On Becoming a Leader*, Business Books 1989.
Mant, A. *Leaders We Deserve*. Martin Robertson 1983.
   A wonderfully idiosyncratic book by an Australian with a psychological bent and a perceptive view of British ways.
Cooper, C. & Hingley, P. *The Change Makers*. Harper & Row 1985.
   Some good interviews with leading British men and women on what shaped their lives and their thinking.
Peters, T. *Thriving on Chaos*. Harper & Row 1987.
   Good for upside-down thinking. Another enjoyable and challenging book by one of the authors of *In Search of Excellence*.

Chapter Six:
Duffy, M. *Gor-Saga*. Methuen 1981.
   A fictional view of the world ahead. Worrying.

Chapter Seven:
Kolb, D. *Experimental Learning*. Prentice Hall 1984.
   The best exposition of how adults learn that I know of.
Argyris, C. & Schon, D. *Organizational Learning: A Theory in Action Perspective*. Addison Wesley 1978.
   A bit academic in tone but an important book for anyone who wants to move beyond training to learning in an organization.
Revans, R.W. *The Origins and Growth of Action Learning*. Chartwell Bratt 1982.
   The great prophet of action learning explains its history and its rationale.
Dewey, J. *Democracy & Educating*. Free Press 1916.
   A classic book for all liberal-minded educationalists.
Illich, I. *Deschooling Society*. Penguin 1971.
   A radical attack on educational tradition.
Harvey-Jones, J. *Making It Happen. Reflections on Leadership*. Collins 1988.
   A splendid and readable account of how one man, in my view anyway, changed a corporate culture, that of ICI in Britain.
Kanter, R.M. *The Change Masters: Corporate Entrepreneurs at Work*. Allen & Unwin 1981.
   An account of how and why companies change or do not change. Very authoritative. Also, her latest book *When Giants Learn to Dance*, Simon & Schuster 1989.
Mumford, A.L. et al. *Developing Directors: The Learning Process*. Manpower Services Commission 1987.
   A short account of how Britain's top managers learnt or did not learn as they progressed.
Gardner, H. *Frames of Mind*. Heinemann 1983.
   One of those important books which are difficult to read at times, but can change your whole way of thinking, in this case on intelligence and on education.

Index

THE EMPTY RAINCOAT

Charles Handy

'Life will never be easy, or sure, or perfect. Best understood backwards, we have to live it forwards – with all its contradictions. There is a paradox at the heart of things. The challenge of the future is to find a pathway through the paradoxes.'

* Are you on the way to Davy's Bar?
* When is the moment to take the Sigmoid Curve?
* Do you know the Doughnut Principle?
* What is a Chinese contract?

The changes which Charles Handy, Britain's foremost business guru, foresaw in *The Age of Unreason* are happening. Endless growth can create a candyfloss economy, and capitalism must be its own sternest critic.

Charles Handy reaches here for a philosophy beyond the mechanics of business organisations, beyond material choices, to try to establish an alternative universe, where life and work are re-grounded in a natural sense of continuity, connection and purposeful direction.

THE GODS OF MANAGEMENT

Charles Handy

The four gods of the title symbolise the very different styles of management and culture to be found in today's organisations. Zeus is the dynamic entrepreneur who rules over companies of the **club culture**, characterised by speed of decision and rapid, intuitive communication. Apollo, god of order and bureaucracy, is the patron of the **role culture**, based not on personalities but on definition of the jobs to be done. Athena, goddess of craftsmen, recognises only expertise as the basis of power and influence: hers is the **task culture**. Dionysus is the god preferred by artists and professionals within the **existential culture**, people who owe little or no allegiance to a boss.

Under the witty and sparkling allegory Charles Handy, Britain's foremost business guru, makes a serious analysis of the changing patterns of work and business. Management is not a precise science but has aspects of a creative and political process which is influenced by the prevailing culture and traditions of the organisation. His theme is illustrated with a wealth of case studies and examples drawn from business around the world.

This book is a world bestseller which is required reading for managers, business students and everyone who wants to be a survivor in a world of constantly changing organisational culture.

BEYOND CERTAINTY

Charles Handy

'. . . remarkably fresh and stimulating – a radical and articulate call to shape our own futures in uncertain times, without allowing the past to stand in the way'
John Plender, *RSA Journal*

Over the last decade, change has accelerated violently. The Thatcher/Reagan years were a time of certainty, when greed was good, more meant better, and the Western world rejoiced to see George Orwell's dismal prophecy for 1984 confounded. But there is a curvilinear logic in the universe. Prosperity cannot last for ever.

Empires and organisations must flounder. The world must be reinvented. We can now be certain only of uncertainty. Compromise may be the way forward, and organisations must give more freedom to individuals to preserve commitment and creativity.

In this challenging and exhilarating collection of pieces, Charles Handy, Britain's foremost business guru, takes us on an intellectual journey through a changing world, in order to see how we must adapt to make our future work.

MAVERICK

Ricardo Semler

The success story behind the world's most unusual
workplace.

'Irresistibly stimulating'
Robert Heller

'The way that Ricardo Semler runs his company is
impossible; except that it works splendidly for everyone.
I relish this book. It revived my faith in human beings
and my hope for businesses elsewhere'
Charles Handy

'Semco takes a workplace democracy to previously
unimagined frontiers'
The Times

'His egalitarian approach works like a dream'
Today

The international bestseller that tells how Semler tore up
the rule books – and defied inflation running at up to
900% per year!

* Workers make the decisions previously made by their
  bosses
* Managerial staff set their own salaries and bonuses
* Everyone has access to the company books
* No formality – a minimum of meetings, memos,
  approvals
* Internal walls torn down
* Shopfloor workers set their own productivity targets
  and schedules
* Result – Semco is one of Latin America's fastest-
  growing companies, acknowledged to be the best in
  Brazil to work for, and with a waiting list of
  thousands of applicants hoping to join it.

THE ROAD LESS TRAVELLED

M. Scott Peck

A new psychology of love, traditional values and spiritual growth.

Confronting and solving problems is a painful process which most of us attempt to avoid. And the very avoidance results in greater pain and an inability to grow both mentally and spiritually. Drawing heavily on his own professional experience, Dr M. Scott Peck, a practising psychiatrist, suggests ways in which facing our difficulties – and suffering through the changes – can enable us to reach a higher level of self-understanding. He discusses the nature of loving relationships: how to recognize true compatibility; how to distinguish dependency from love: how to become one's own person and how to be a more sensitive parent.

This book is a phenomenon. Continuously on the US bestseller list for five years, it will change your life.

'Magnificent . . . This is not just a book, but a spontaneous act of generosity written by author who leans towards the reader for the purpose of sharing something larger than himself'
Washington

EXPLORING THE ROAD LESS TRAVELLED

Alice & Walden Howard
Foreword by M. Scott Peck

A practical companion guide and teachers' manual for those who wish to study further, in groups or as individuals, the challenging ideas outlined by psychiatrist Dr M. Scott Peck in his world-wide bestseller *The Road Less Travelled*.

Dr Peck's argument that we need a 'new psychology of love, traditional values and spiritual growth' has found a wide and receptive audience and thousands of study groups have been formed to explore his ideas in greater depth. To aid them, Alice and Walden Howard have prepared this manual. It is a book for teachers, educationalists, psychiatrists, social and community workers, ministers of religion, spiritual counsellors and, indeed, everyone seeking a way out of the stresses and tensions of today's violent and fragmented world.

WHAT RETURN CAN I MAKE?

M. Scott Peck
Dimensions of the Christian Experience

'The Lord is my light and my salvation'

This most unusual book celebrates the Christian message in music and hymns composed by Sister Marilyn Von Waldner, drawings by Patricia Kay, and essays on aspects of Christian belief by Dr M. Scott Peck. The essays, thematically related to the hymns, deal with topics such as Grace, Guilt, Faith and Communion. Dr Scott Peck brings to the essays spiritual insights which have come to him during the course of his psychiatric work and as a result of his encountering the music and songs of Sister Marilyn. No reader will remain unmoved by their inspiring, rewarding and challenging collaboration.

THE DIFFERENT DRUM

M. Scott Peck

The Creation of True Community – the First Step to World Peace

'The overall purpose of human communication is – or should be – reconciliation. It should ultimately serve to lower or remove the walls of misunderstanding which unduly separate us human beings, one from another . . .'

Although we have developed the technology to make communication more efficient and to bring people closer together, we have failed to use it to build a true, global community.

Dr M. Scott Peck believes that if we are to prevent civilization destroying itself, we must urgently rebuild community at all levels, local, national and international, and that is the first step to spiritual survival.

In this radical and challenging book he describes how the communities work, how group action can be developed and the principles of tolerance and love, and how we can start to transform world society into a true community.

'I have been touched by this inspiring book'
Carly Simon

LOVE, MEDICINE AND MIRACLES

Bernie S. Siegel M.D.

This remarkable book contains the lessons about self-healing, written by a doctor who has watched 'terminal' patients take control of their illness and live.

'We do have biological "live" and "die" mechanisms within us . . . the state of mind changes the state of the body by working through the central nervous system, the endocrine system and the immune system. Exceptional patients manifest the will to live in its most potent form . . . writes Dr Bernie Siegal. Through the healing power of love, patients who have come under his care have learned to change, enrich and prolong their lives beyond medical expectation.

None of us can know when illness will strike us or those we love, but we *can* do something about it. *Love, Medicine and Miracles* shows us how.

'A wonderful book that every patient and sceptic physician should read'
Elizabeth Kubler Ross

'His book is, and will be, a blessing to all humanity"
Dr Carl Simonton

OTHER TITLES AVAILABLE IN ARROW

ALL ARROW BOOKS ARE AVAILABLE THROUGH MAIL ORDER OR FROM YOUR LOCAL BOOKSHOP.

PAYMENT MAY BE MADE USING ACCESS, VISA, MASTER-CARD, DINERS CLUB, SWITCH AND AMEX, OR CHEQUE, EUROCHEQUE AND POSTAL ORDER (STERLING ONLY).

EXPIRY DATE .... SWITCH ISSUE NO.

SIGNATURE...

PLEASE ALLOW £2.50 FOR POST AND PACKING FOR THE FIRST BOOK AND £1.00 PER BOOK THEREAFTER.

ORDER TOTAL: £ .... (INCLUDING P&P)

ALL ORDERS TO:
ARROW BOOKS, BOOKS BY POST, TBS LIMITED, THE BOOK SERVICE, COLCHESTER ROAD, FRATING GREEN, COLCHESTER, ESSEX, CO7 7DW, UK.
TELEPHONE: (01206) 256 000
FAX: (01206) 255 914

NAME: ....

ADDRESS ....

....

Please allow 28 days for delivery. Please tick box if you do not wish to receive any additional information ❑
Prices and availability subject to change without notice.

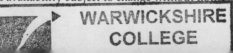